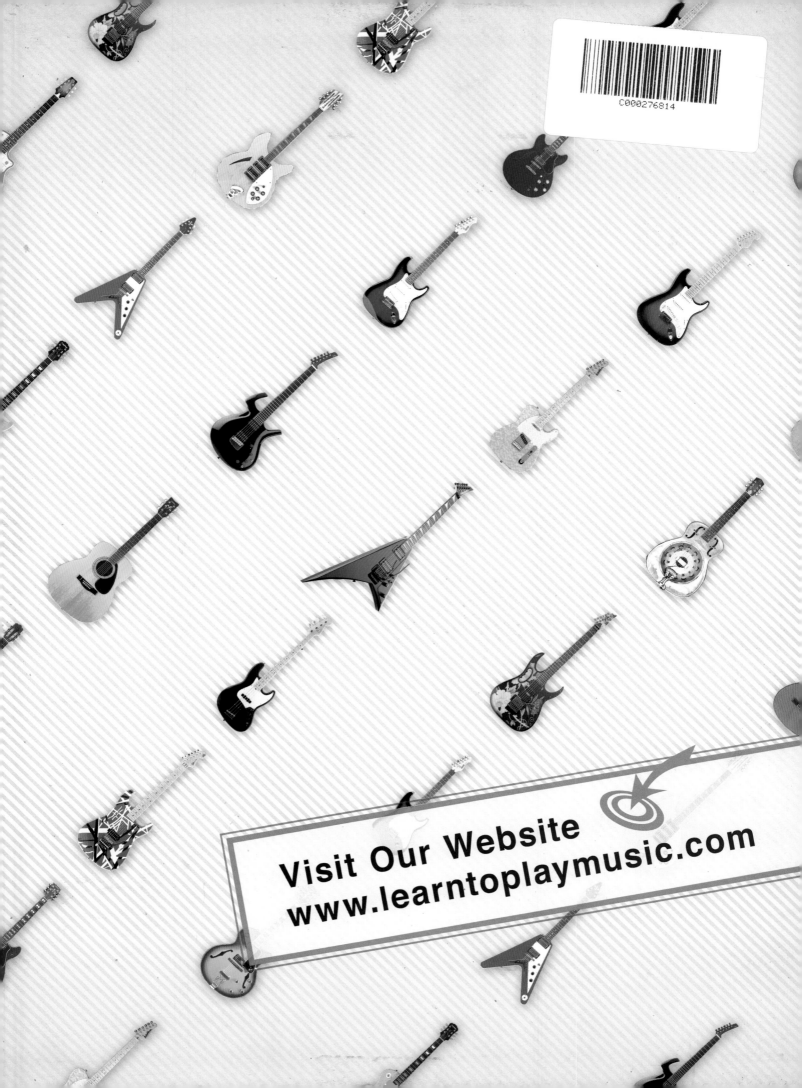

Visit Our Website
www.learntoplaymusic.com

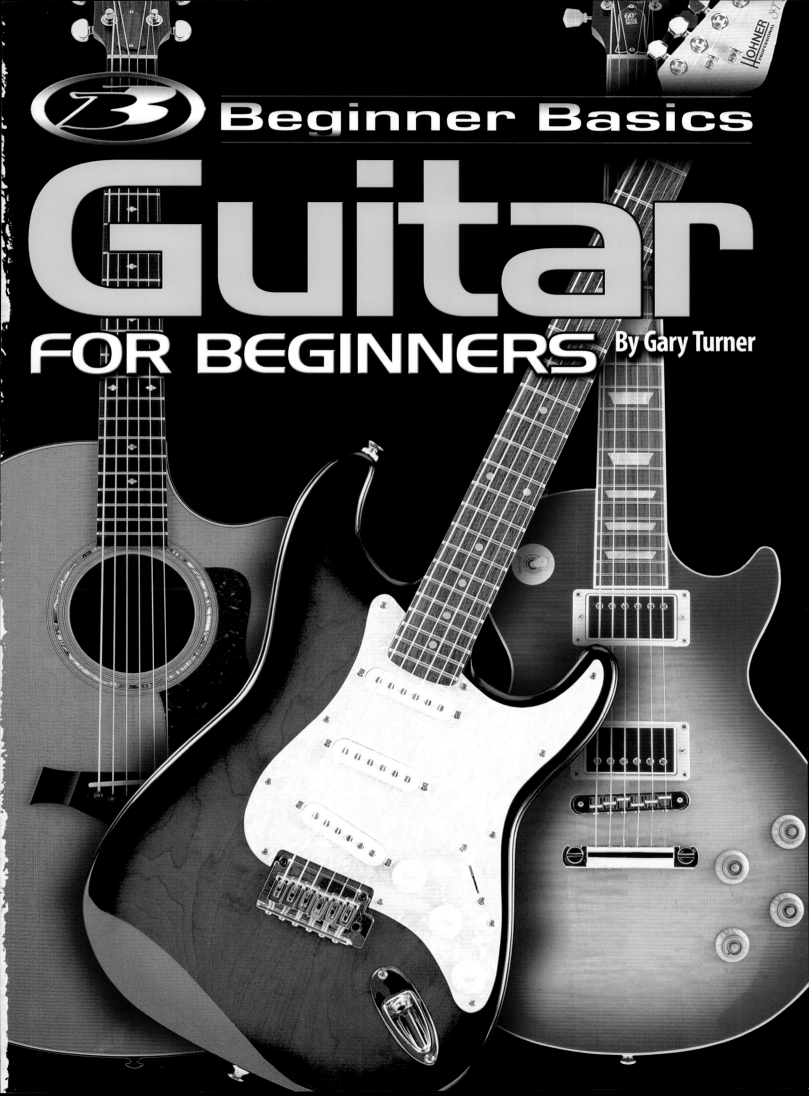

BEGINNER BASICS GUITAR
I.S.B.N. 978-982-9118-14-1
Order Code: 11814

For more information on the
Learn to Play series contact:
L.T.P. Publishing Pty Ltd
email: info@learntoplaymusic.com
or visit our website:
www.learntoplaymusic.com

Published by
KOALA MUSIC PUBLICATIONS ™

Contents

Introduction

Beginner Basics Guitar assumes you have no prior knowledge of music or playing the GUITAR.

Starting from the types of guitar available and the different styles of playing you are introduced to :

1. Important basic chord shapes and chord progressions.
2. Learn to read and play guitar music using standard music notation, **EASY READ TAB** and **EASY READ strumming patterns** and **chord diagrams.**
3. Learn to play the notes on all six strings.
4. Learn the melodies and chords of over 20 well known songs and chord progressions including Rock, Blues and Turnaround Progressions.
5. Learn basic music theory including time signatures, sharps and flats, major scales etc.
6. Learn the most common open chord shapes in the keys of C major, G major and A minor.

The book also has special sections on tuning, how to read sheet music of your favourite groups, and a chord chart.

After completing this book you will have a solid understanding of the guitar and will be ready for further study on specific styles of guitar playing.

*   If you want to learn more about chords and rhythms, see **Complete Learn To Play Rhythm Guitar Manual**.
*   If you want to learn more about lead guitar and improvising, see **Complete Learn To Play Lead Guitar Manual**.
*   If you want to learn more about fingerpicking with the right hand, see **Complete Learn To Play Fingerpicking Guitar Manual**.

ALL GUITARISTS SHOULD KNOW ALL OF THE INFORMATION CONTAINED IN THIS BOOK

The best and fastest way to learn is to use this book in conjunction with:

1. Buying sheet music and song books of your favourite recording artists and learning to play their songs.
2. Practicing and playing with other musicians. You will be surprised how good a basic drums/bass/guitar combination can sound even when playing easy music.
3. Learning by listening to your favourite CDs.

Also in the early stages it is helpful to have the guidance of an experienced teacher. This will also help you keep to a schedule and obtain weekly goals.

Motivation and Learning

Anybody can play a musical instrument.

Everyone is born with the natural talents and gifts required to play a musical instrument. Whether they succeed and how well they will be able to play depends upon several factors. Any one factor alone is not enough. Whether you become an average, good or brilliant musician depends on how much you are able to apply each the following:

1. Aptitude and Natural Abilities - Make the most of your natural talent - it's too valuable to waste. Being born with natural ability is not enough. No matter how much ability you are born with, unless you are dedicated, persevere and practice, you will not become a good musician. The natural abilities some are born with will help determine which instrument they will be most proficient at. Some people have abilities which allow them to become virtuosos in one particular instrument, while others excel with almost any instrument they play. Some may only shine with the instrument they are most interested in.

2. Desire Attitude and Motivation - If you want to become a good musician you can. For a young person making it fun and having a sense of pride and achievement is very important to create and retain a desire to continue learning. If a child is forced to learn an instrument they don't enjoy, or if they are not encouraged and supported with their musical progress, they will lose interest and ultimately give up. For the older student the desire to learn is a starting point. You have to want something to achieve it.

3. Objectives and Goals - If you don't know where you want to be how can you get there? If you dream where you want to be, you can visualize it and take the right steps to get there.

4. Dedication and Commitment - If you always try to the best of your abilities you will become the best musician you can be. If you only make half the effort you will only achieve half your potential. A person without natural ability but with a desire to play, through dedication, perseverance and practice, can become a better musician than someone with great natural ability who is unmotivated.

5. Patience and Perseverance - Don't give up when things become difficult and you will succeed. If you have the will power to succeed you will succeed. Whilst you are learning there might be stages where your progress is slow. With perseverance you will always overcome these hurdles.

6. Practice Practice Practice - Practice is proportional to success. The more you practice the better you will become. It's important to practice 'smart'. Your progress will be faster with regular short sessions, rather than one long weekly session.
Just do it and keep doing it! Every day!

Am I too old to start learning?

You are never too old to start to learning a musical instrument. Whether you are 3 or 93, if you have the desire and dedication, you will be able to play. By combining the above six factors with desire and commitment you will become a great musician.

  www.learntoplaymusic.com

Approach to Practice

From the beginning you should set yourself a goal. Many people learn guitar because of a desire to play like their favourite artist (e.g. Eric Clapton), or to play a certain style of music (e.g. Rock, Blues etc.). Motivations such as these will help you to persevere through the more difficult sections of work. As you develop, it will be important to adjust and update your goals.

It is important to have a correct approach to practice. You will benefit more from several short practices (e.g. 15-30 minutes per day) than one or two long sessions per week. This is especially so in the early stages, because of the basic nature of the material being studied.

In a practice session you should divide your time evenly between the study of new material and the revision of past work. It is a common mistake for semi-advanced students to practice only the pieces they can already play well. Although this is more enjoyable, it is not a very satisfactory method of practice.

You should also try to correct mistakes and experiment with new ideas. It is the author's belief that an experienced teacher will be an invaluable aid to your progress.

Choosing a Guitar

The type of guitar you choose to play will depend largely on the style of music you are intending to play. Many beginners start on a nylon string guitar because they are the cheapest and easiest to play. However, by the time you have achieved a basic proficiency on the guitar, you will be ready to choose an instrument suited to the music you like to play.

If you play Classical, Folk or Flamenco, a nylon string guitar is perfectly suited to these styles, although Folk guitarists may also use a steel string acoustic. If you play Acoustic Blues, Country, Bluegrass, Ragtime or World music, you would probably choose a steel string acoustic.

Most Jazz players prefer a hollow body electric guitar, while most Rock and Pop players use solid body electric guitars. Blues, R&B and Funk players may use either type of electric guitar. Before purchasing a guitar, it is recommended that you try out several types and ask an experienced player to demonstrate the pros and cons of each. This way you can make a more informed decision and will end up with a guitar you are happy with.

Using the accompanying DVDs and CDs

The discs included contain video and audio recordings of all of the examples in this book. An exercise number and the symbol below indicates a recorded example.

Exercise 27

CD TRACK/DVD MENU NUMBER

The book shows you where to put your fingers and what technique to use. The recordings let you hear and see how each example should sound and look when performed correctly. Practice the examples slowly at first on your own. Then try playing to a metronome (see page 125) set to a slow tempo such that you can play the example evenly and without stopping the beat. Gradually increase the tempo as you become more confident and then you can try playing along with the recording.

To play along with the CDs and DVDs your guitar must be in tune (see "Tuning Your Guitar" on page 17). If you have tuned using an electronic tuner your guitar will already be in tune. You will hear a drum beat at the beginning of each example, to lead you in and to help you keep time.

Included with this book is:
* **2 DVDs**, which can be played in any DVD player. This disc contains a menu to guide you to the exercises found in the book, and a separate tuning menu.
* **2 CDs** which can be played in any player. The 2nd CD contains all new versions of the original backing tracks so you can play them at different tempos and in different styles.
* **2 DVD-ROMs**, which can be used in any computer and most gaming consoles and portable media players (e.g. iPod, Xbox, Playstation etc). This disc is for use with Microsoft Windows Media Player (included free with all Windows PCs) and for Apple iTunes and Quicktime Media Player (included free with all Apple Macintosh computers and available for Windows PCs via free download at www.apple.com). On this disc you will find 2 folders, one containing the video examples and the other containing the audio examples. There is also 2 audio folders, 1 folder contains the full mix of each example, while the second folder contains brand new backing mixes without the lead part. Follow the instructions for your media player to import these files to your hard drive and transfer to your portable media player if required.

TIPS
* Most DVDs and portable media players have the ability to repeat tracks. You can make good use of this feature to practice the examples a number of times without stopping.
* The latest versions of both Windows Media Player and Quicktime Player (available with iTunes) have the ability to slow down the speed of the recorded exercises while still maintaining the correct pitch . This is very handy for practicing the more complex pieces.

History of the Guitar

Stringed instruments have existed since ancient times and are used in almost every culture. Some important forerunners of the guitar are the **Lute** and the **Oud**, both of which originated in the middle east. These instruments have four or five courses of two strings side by side - similar to a mandolin or a twelve string guitar.

The guitar itself first appeared in **Spain** in about the **15th century**. The first guitars were variations on the lute, which was one of the most popular Renaissance instruments. These guitars had four or five courses of strings. In the 16th century, the first published music for the guitar was written by Alonso Mudarra. His pieces are still played by guitarists today. Towards the end of the 18th century, the first six string guitar appeared. This was a much more versatile instrument than the earlier versions and its popularity quickly spread throughout Europe and eventually to all parts of the world.

The first half of the 19th century is the period of greatest development of **Classical guitar** music. There were several guitar virtuosos at this time who wrote prolifically for the instrument. The most famous of these were Fernando Sor, Dionisio Aguado, Matteo Carcassi and Mauro Giuliani. On hearing Giuliani perform, Beethoven is reputed to have said "the guitar is a miniature orchestra in itself".

The Classical guitar and it's repertoire have continued to develop up to the present day. The modern Classical guitar is larger than earlier versions and gut strings have been replaced by nylon, but the sound and techniques are basically the same.

The **steel string Acoustic guitar** developed in **America**. German born luthier (guitar maker) **C.F. Martin** developed an cross brace under the soundboard to strengthen the guitar and when steel strings first appeared around 1900, this design was perfectly suited to the extra tension the steel strings put on the guitar. The Martin company is still probably the most famous of all acoustic guitar makers but today there are many variations on the basic design of the steel string guitar. Some of these include the Resonator guitar which contains a metal resonator cone and is frequently used for slide guitar, the Lap steel guitar and the 12 string guitar.

The **Electric guitar** was invented in the 1930's by **Adolph Rickenbacker** and George Beauchamp. The first electric guitars were basically amplified acoustic guitars, mainly used by Jazz guitarists, but throughout the following decades the designs began to change. In the 1950's, **solid body electric guitars** began to appear. The most famous of these were the **Fender Stratocaster** and the **Gibson Les Paul.** These guitars rely on the pickups and amplifier to produce the sound of the guitar, whereas hollow body electric guitars such as the Gibson 125 or 175 use a combination of acoustic and electric sounds. Another important part of modern electric guitars is the **tremolo arm** or 'whammy bar' which is used to produce a variety of sounds, from subtle vibrato to dramatic space age sounds. Today's electric guitars come in a vast array of shapes, sizes, colours and pickup configurations.

Acoustic Guitars

CLASSICAL [Nylon Strings] ACOUSTIC [Steel Strings] CLASSICAL CUTAWAY ACOUSTIC CUTAWAY

The **CLASSICAL GUITAR** has nylon strings and a wider neck than other types of guitar. It is most commonly used for playing Classical, Flamenco and Fingerstyle. Generally it is much cheaper than other types of guitar and is recommended for beginning guitarists.
The **STEEL STRING ACOUSTIC** has steel strings and is most commonly played by strumming or fingerpicking groups of notes called chords. This is the type of acoustic guitar you will hear in most modern styles of music such as Top 40 Rock and Pop music.

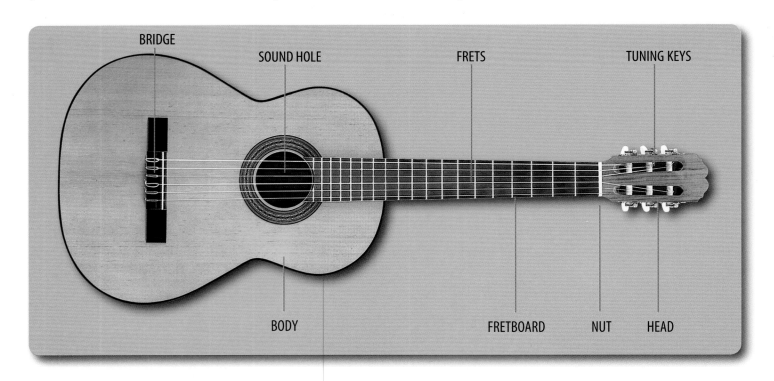

Electric Guitars

SOLID BODY ELECTRIC   SOLID BODY ELECTRIC   HOLLOWBODY ELECTRIC   ELECTRIC 12 STRING

Electric guitars have **pick-ups** (a type of inbuilt microphone) and need to be plugged into an **amplifier** (amp) to be heard. The **solid body electric** is commonly used in Metal, Rock, Blues and Pop Music. Famous solid body guitars are the **Gibson Les Paul** and the **Fender Stratocaster**. The **hollow body electric** (semi acoustic) is most commonly used in Jazz and Blues music. Acoustic guitars can be amplified by using a microphone placed near the sound hole or by placing a portable pick-up on the body of the guitar.

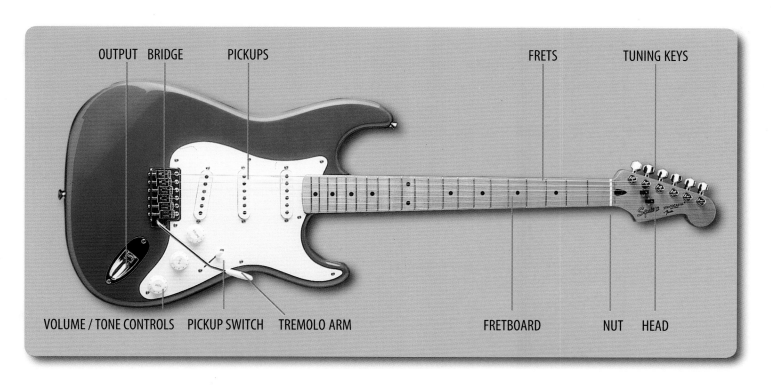

OUTPUT   BRIDGE   PICKUPS   FRETS   TUNING KEYS

VOLUME / TONE CONTROLS   PICKUP SWITCH   TREMOLO ARM   FRETBOARD   NUT   HEAD

Strings

It is important to have the correct set of strings fitted to your guitar, especially if you are a beginner. Until you build enough strength in your hands to fret the chords cleanly, light gauge or low tension strings are recommended.

A reputable music store selling guitar strings should be able to assist with this.

Do not put steel strings on a classical guitar, it will damage the neck of the guitar.

It is important to **change your strings regularly,** as old strings go out of tune easily and are more difficult to keep in tune.

Amplifiers

COMBO
Combined Amp and Speaker

STACK
Separate Amp Head and Speaker

Accessories

Here are some accessories you will need to be familiar with as a guitarist.

PICKS (or PLECTRUMS)

GUITAR STRAPS

ELECTRONIC METRONOME

EFFECTS PEDALS

GUITAR CASE

GUITAR LEADS

Styles of Playing Guitar

The guitar is the most versatile musical instrument and can be used to play virtually all music styles including Classical, Rock, Pop, Blues, Jazz, Country, Funk, Metal, Folk, Rock 'n' Roll etc. There are many different styles of playing guitar and all these styles can be played on any type of guitar. All guitars have six strings and are tuned the same. You would usually play lead on an electric guitar but you could play lead on a classical guitar, or play fingerpicking style on an electric guitar. It all depends upon the sound you are looking for.

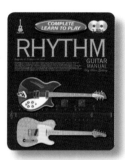

Progressive Complete Rhythm Guitar

Used to accompany a lead instrument (e.g. melody sung by a vocalist). The left hand holds a chord shape (a group of notes) and the right hand strums the strings with a pick.
To learn how to play more chords and rhythms, see
COMPLETE LEARN TO PLAY RHYTHM GUITAR MANUAL

Progressive Complete Lead Guitar

Used to play only one or two notes at a time. It can either be a melody line or an improvised solo. Most lead players use a pick.
To learn how to play lead guitar see
COMPLETE LEARN TO PLAY LEAD GUITAR MANUAL

Progressive Complete Fingerpicking Guitar

The left hand holds a chord shape and the right hand fingers pick one or two notes at a time with the fingernails. Used to accompany a lead instrument or vocalist. To learn how to play fingerpicking guitar see
COMPLETE LEARN TO PLAY FINGERPICKING GUITAR MANUAL

Progressive Complete Classical Guitar

A specific type of fingerpicking, played on nylon string guitars. This style often involves playing melodies, harmonies and bass lines simultaneously. It is best to study Classical guitar with a teacher to ensure that you develop a correct technique. To learn how to play classical guitar, see
COMPLETE LEARN TO PLAY CLASSICAL GUITAR MANUAL

Progressive Slide Guitar

Played with a glass or metal slide (cylinder) worn on the third or fourth finger of the left hand. Slide guitar produces a variety of sounds, from a singing vocal quality to rough percussive sounds. It can be played either fingerstyle or with a pick. To learn how to play slide guitar, see
PROGRESSIVE SLIDE GUITAR

Tuning Your Guitar

The **easiest** and **most accurate** way to tune your guitar is by using an **electronic tuner**. An electronic tuner allows you to tune each string individually, by indicating whether the notes are sharp (too high) or flat (too low).

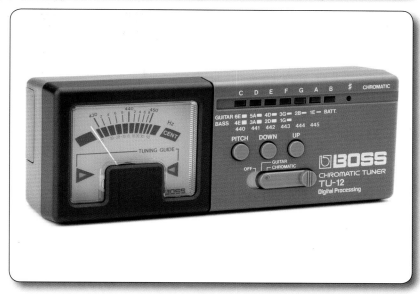

If you have an electric guitar you can plug it directly into the tuner. If you have an acoustic guitar, the tuner will have an inbuilt microphone. There are several types of electronic guitar tuners, most are relatively inexpensive and simple to operate. Tuning using other methods is difficult for beginning guitarists and it takes many months to master, so we **recommend** you purchase an electronic tuner, particularly if you do not have a guitar teacher or a friend who can tune it for you. If your guitar is way out of tune you can always take it to your local music store so they can tune it for you. Once a guitar has been tuned correctly it should only need minor adjustments before each practice session.

For a more in depth look at alternative methods of tuning your guitar please refer to Appendics towards the back of this book. **(from page 102)**

Exercise 1-6

Before you commence each lesson or practice session you will need to tune your guitar. If your guitar is out of tune everything you play will sound incorrect even though you are holding the correct notes. On the accompanying CD, you will find exercises 1-6 which correspond to the **six strings of the guitar**. On the DVD, these are found in the **tuning section** of the DVD menu. **Please refer to page 104 towards the back of this book.**

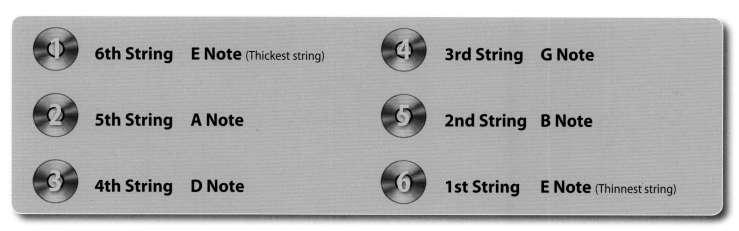

1. **6th String** **E Note** (Thickest string)
2. **5th String** **A Note**
3. **4th String** **D Note**
4. **3rd String** **G Note**
5. **2nd String** **B Note**
6. **1st String** **E Note** (Thinnest string)

How to Read Music

There are two methods used to write guitar music. First is the **traditional music notation** method (using music notes, ♩) and second is **tablature**. Both are used in this book but you need only use one of these methods. Most guitarists find tablature easier to read, however, it is very worthwhile to learn to read traditional music notation as well. Nearly all sheet music you buy in a store is written in traditional notation.

Tablature

Tablature is a method of indicating the position of notes on the fretboard. There are six "tab" lines, each representing one of the six strings of the guitar. Study the following diagram.

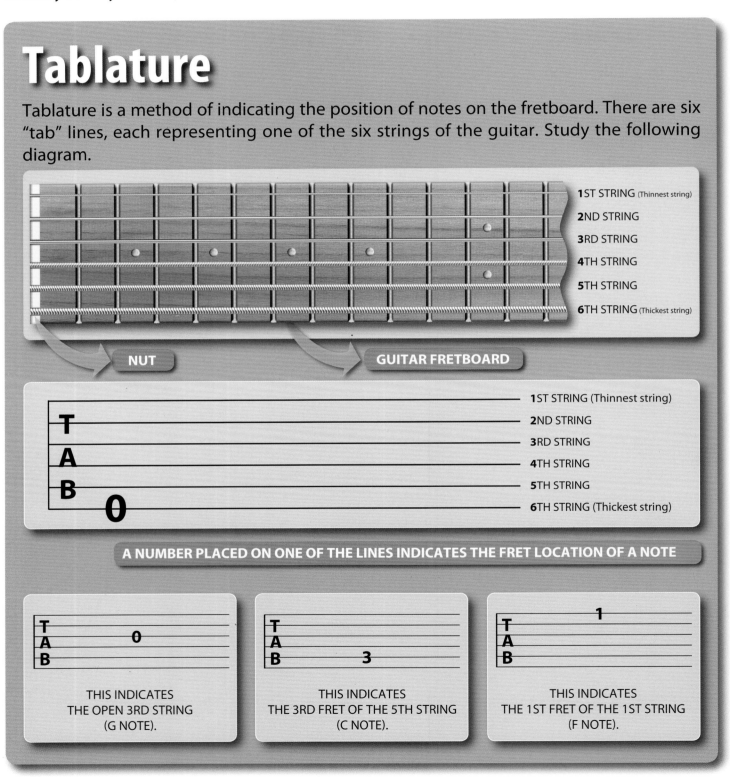

1ST STRING (Thinnest string)
2ND STRING
3RD STRING
4TH STRING
5TH STRING
6TH STRING (Thickest string)

NUT · GUITAR FRETBOARD

1ST STRING (Thinnest string)
2ND STRING
3RD STRING
4TH STRING
5TH STRING
6TH STRING (Thickest string)

A NUMBER PLACED ON ONE OF THE LINES INDICATES THE FRET LOCATION OF A NOTE

THIS INDICATES
THE OPEN 3RD STRING
(G NOTE).

THIS INDICATES
THE 3RD FRET OF THE 5TH STRING
(C NOTE).

THIS INDICATES
THE 1ST FRET OF THE 1ST STRING
(F NOTE).

Music Notation

STAFF

These five lines are called the **staff** or the **stave**.

Fourth Space → ... ← Fifth Line
Third Space → ... ← Fourth Line
Second Space → ... ← Middle Line
First Space → ... ← Second Line
... ← First Line

THE TREBLE CLEF

This symbol is called a **treble clef**. There is a treble clef at the beginning of every line of guitar music.

MUSIC NOTES

There are only seven letters used for notes in music.

They are: **A B C D E F G**

These notes are known as the **musical alphabet**. Guitar music notes are written in the spaces and on the lines of the treble staff.

THE TREBLE STAFF

A staff with a treble clef written on it is called a **treble staff**.

THE QUARTER NOTE

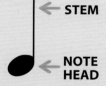

STEM

NOTE HEAD

This music note is called a **quarter note**. A quarter note lasts for **one beat**.

NOTES AND REST VALUES

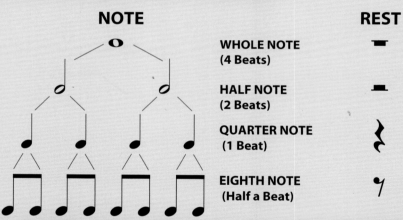

NOTE   REST

WHOLE NOTE (4 Beats)

HALF NOTE (2 Beats)

QUARTER NOTE (1 Beat)

EIGHTH NOTE (Half a Beat)

E G B D F   F A C E

To remember the notes on the lines of the staff:
Every **G**ood **B**oy **D**eserves **F**ruit.

The notes in the spaces spell:
F A C E

Music Notation

THE FOUR FOUR TIME SIGNATURE

This time signature is called the **four four time signature**. It indicates there are **four** beats in each bar. There are four quarter notes in one bar of $\frac{4}{4}$ time.

When playing in $\frac{4}{4}$ time, it is possible to use any combination of note values which add up to the equivalent of four quarter notes. As you progress through the book, you will learn how to use Whole, Half, Quarter and Eighth notes. These are the most common note values used in music.

BARS AND MEASURES

BAR LINES are drawn across the staff, which divides the music into sections called **BARS** or **MEASURES**. A **DOUBLE BAR LINE** signifies either the end of the music, or the end of an important section of it.

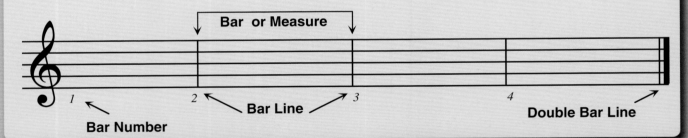

$\frac{4}{4}$ is the most common time signature and is sometimes represented by this symbol called **common time**.

Section 1
Guitar Basics

How to Hold the Guitar

Sitting

1 Sit up straight on the front part of the chair as shown in the photo.
2 Raise your right leg by crossing it over your left leg or by placing your right foot on a footstool (as shown in the adjacent photo). Then place your guitar on your right leg.
3 The guitar should be close to your body in an upright position, with the neck pointing slightly upwards.

The main aim is to be comfortable and have easy access to the guitar fretboard. A music stand will also be helpful.

Standing

1 Use a wide guitar strap and adjust it to a comfortable length. Let the strap take the weight of the guitar. This will keep your hands free to play rather than having to support the instrument.
2 Make sure your weight is balanced evenly between both feet.
3 The guitar should sit comfortably against your body in an upright position, with the neck pointing slightly upwards.

The standing position is particularly good for playing electric guitar and is essential if you plan to play in a band. Once you are comfortable with this position, try moving in time with the music as you play.

Right Hand & Arm

Using the Pick

The **right hand** is used to play the strings by plucking them with a pick. A pick is a piece of plastic shaped like a triangle.

Hold the pick lightly between your **thumb and first finger**, as shown in the following photo.

Use the tip of the pick to play the string.

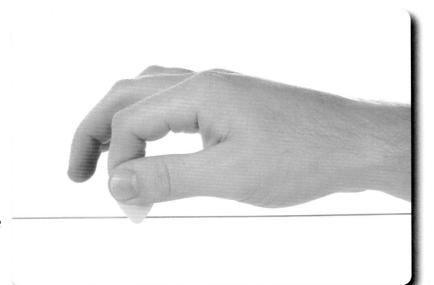

Right Arm Position

The correct position for your right arm is shown in the photos right. Notice that your forearm rests on the upper edge of the guitar, just below the elbow. Be careful not to have your elbow hanging over the face of the guitar, or your right hand too far along the fretboard. Also, when you are playing single notes, support your right hand by placing the third and fourth fingers on the body of the guitar.

If you are playing an **acoustic** guitar, pick the strings over the sound hole, as this makes the best sound.

If you are playing an **electric** guitar, pick the strings between the pick-ups.

If you are strumming a chord, do not support your right hand with your fingers on the body of the guitar, but remember to rest your forearm on the upper edge of the body.

Picking over the sound hole

Picking between the pickups

Left Hand & Arm

Left Hand Fingers

The left hand fingers are numbered as such:

Left Hand Placement

Your fingers should be **ON THEIR TIPS** and placed just **BEHIND** the frets (not on top of them).

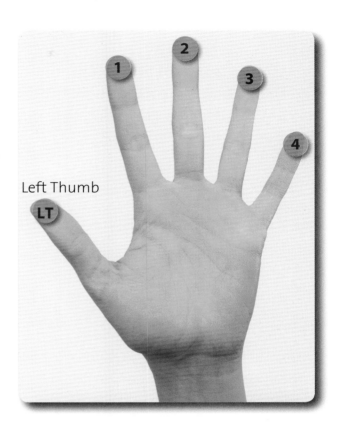

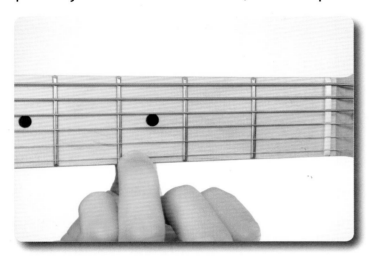

Be careful not to allow the thumb to hang too far over the top of the neck **(Photo A)**, or to let it run parallel along the back of the neck **(Photo B)**.

CORRECT

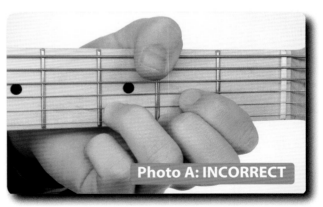

Photo A: INCORRECT

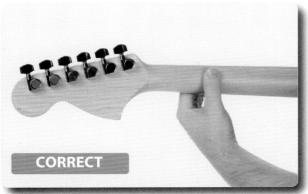

CORRECT

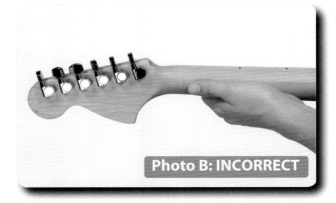

Photo B: INCORRECT

Lesson 1

Chords

A **chord** is a group of three or more notes that are played together. Chords are used to accompany a singer, or an instrumentalist who is playing the melody of a song. The first chord you will learn is the **G major chord**, usually just called the **G chord**.

Major chords are the most common chords. The G major chord is indicated by the letter **G**. This is called the **chord symbol**.

> Before commencing each lesson or practice session, make sure that your guitar is in tune. See page **17** to learn how to tune the guitar.

Chord Diagrams

Chords are learnt with the help of a **chord diagram**. This will show you exactly where to place your left hand fingers in order to play a particular chord. A chord diagram is a grid of horizontal and vertical lines representing the strings and frets of the guitar, as shown below:

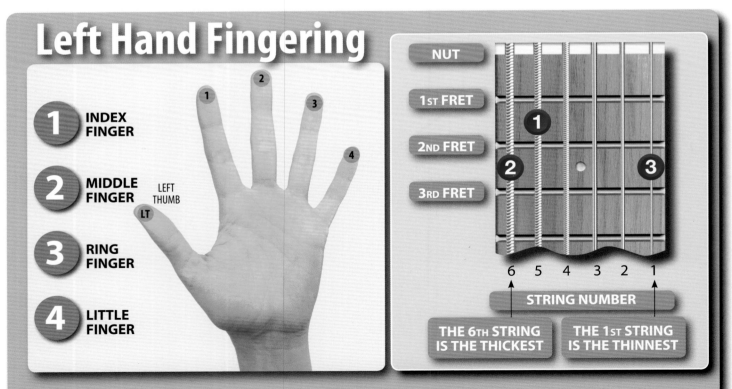

The **COLORED** dots show you where to place your left hand fingers.
The **WHITE** number tells you which finger to place down on the string, just behind the fret. If there is no dot on a string, you play it as an open (not fretted) string.

G Major Chord

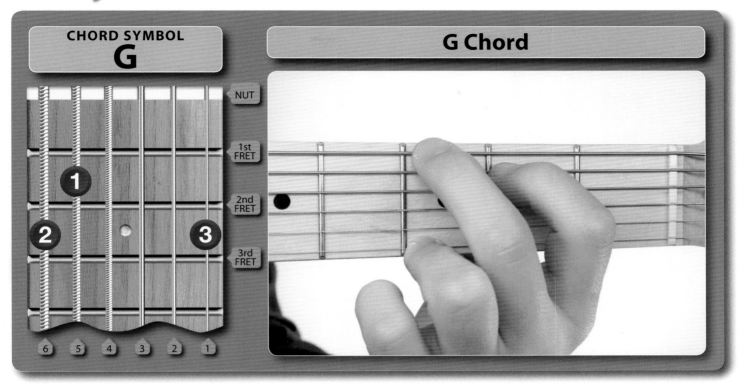

CHORD SYMBOL
G

G Chord

NUT

1st FRET

2nd FRET

3rd FRET

① ② ③

6 5 4 3 2 1

To play the **G** chord place your:
First finger ① just behind the **second** fret of the **5th** string.
Second finger ② just behind the **third** fret of the **6th** string.
Third finger ③ just behind the **third** fret of the **1st** string.

Play **all six strings** with the pick at the same time using a downward motion. This is called a **strum**. Hold the pick lightly and strum from the wrist. Keep your wrist relaxed.

V

Count: 1

This is the **symbol** for a **downward strum.**
This is a **quarter note strum.** It lasts for **one beat**.
There are four quarter note strums in one bar of 4/4 time.
If any notes buzz or sound muffled, you may have to press harder.
Make sure your fingers are just behind the frets.

CHORD SYMBOL

G

The **chord symbol** is written above the staff.
A new chord symbol is placed at the beginning of each bar.

In **exercise 7**, there are four bars of **G** chords. Strum the **G** chord four times for each bar. To make the example sound finished, always end with one strum of the first chord. To help you keep time, play the first strum of each bar louder. The two dots at the end of the staff (before the double bar lines) are called a **repeat sign** and mean that you play the exercise again from the start.

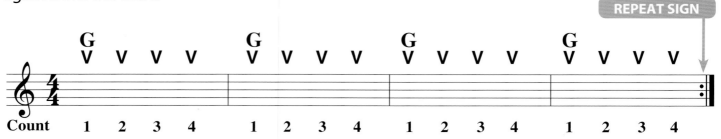

The Seventh Chord

Another type of common chord is called the **dominant seventh** chord. It is usually referred to as the **"seventh"** chord.

The chord symbol for the seventh chord is the number **7** written after the alphabetical letter. The symbol for the **D seventh** chord is **D7**.

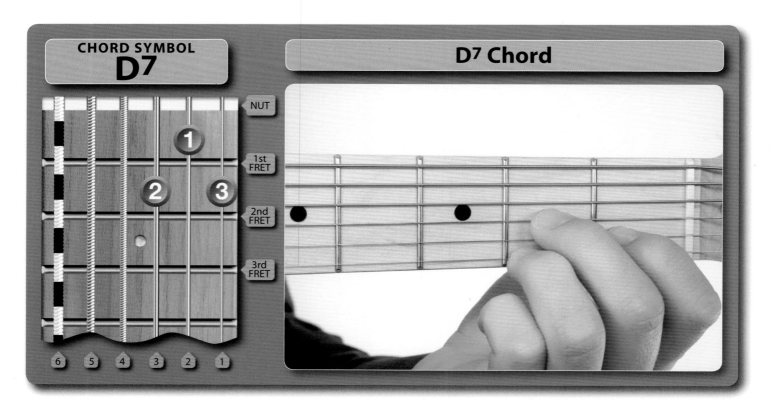

To play the **D7** chord, use the first **three** fingers of your left hand as shown in the diagram, but strum only **five** strings. Do not strum the **6th** string (as indicated by the dotted line). The green colored dots indicate the chord has a dominant function.

Changing from G to D7

The following exercise contains the **G** and **D7** chords.
Practice slowly and evenly, and count or tap your foot as you play (to help you keep time).
There are four strums in each bar.
These chord exercises are called **chord progressions**.

When strumming, only your wrist should move.
Do not move your arm, and keep your forearm resting on the upper edge of the guitar.

Remember to keep your left hand fingers just behind the frets. If you place them on top of the frets, the notes will sound deadened. If you place them too far back from the frets, the notes will buzz and you will have to press down too hard to prevent it.

If you have an acoustic guitar, pick the string over the soundhole as this results in the best sound.

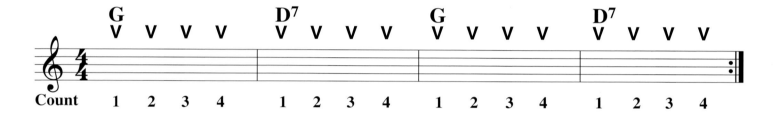

Slide Finger

When changing from **G** to **D7**, do not lift your third finger off the string, but slide it down to the second fret.
Only touch the string very lightly as you do this.
When changing from **D7** to **G**, slide your third finger up to the third fret.
This technique is known as a **slide finger**. It is very useful when changing between chords as it helps you achieve a smoother sound. Practice it many times at a slow tempo (speed) until you can do it automatically.

Look for the possibility of using a slide finger when changing between any two chords.

Lesson 2

Notes on the 3rd String

The G Note

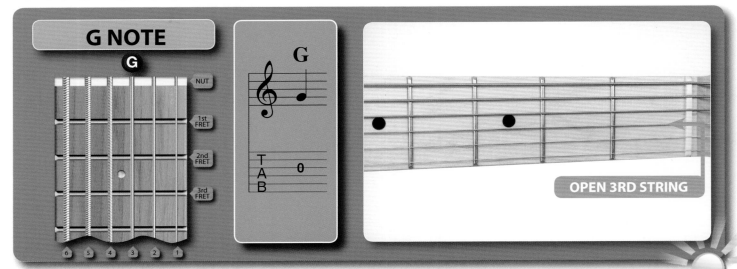

To play the note **G** pick the open **3rd string** (no fingers placed behind frets).

G An open string note is indicated by a **white** letter on a **black** dot.

The A Note

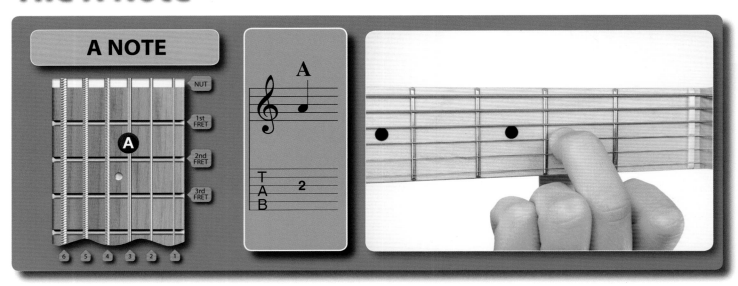

To play the note **A** place the **second finger** of your left hand just behind the second fret of the **3rd string**.

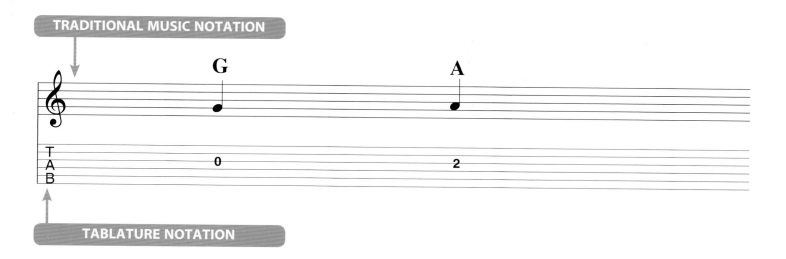

The following chord progression contains two bars of the **note G** followed by two bars of the **note A**. There are **four quarter notes** in each bar.

Remember that you can choose to read the traditional music notation (top line of music), or the Tablature (second line).

To make the example sound finished, end with one strum of the first chord, a **G** chord.

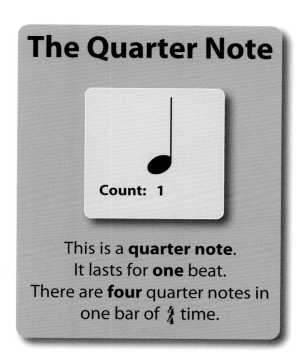

The Quarter Note

Count: 1

This is a **quarter note**. It lasts for **one** beat. There are **four** quarter notes in one bar of $\frac{4}{4}$ time.

Exercise 9

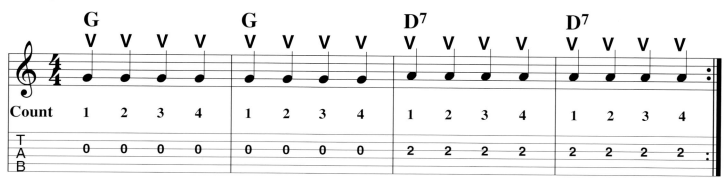

Lesson 3

Notes on the 2nd String

The B Note

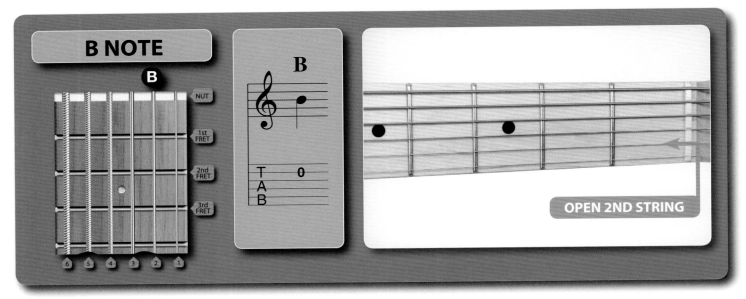

To play the note **B** pick the open **2nd string** (no fingers placed behind frets).

The C Note

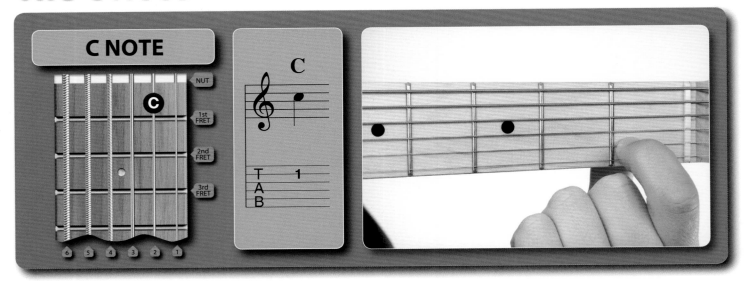

Play the **C** note with the **first finger** of your left hand just behind the **first fret** of the **2nd string** .

The D Note

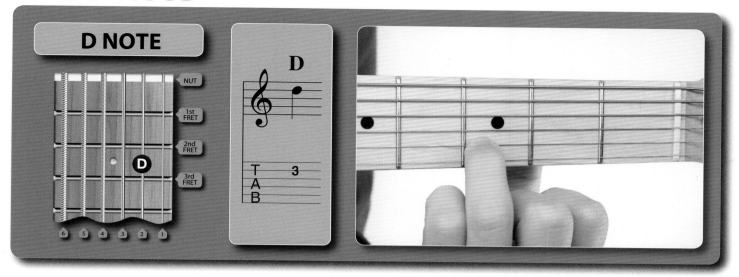

Play the **D** note with the **third finger** of your left hand just behind the **third fret** of the **2nd string**.

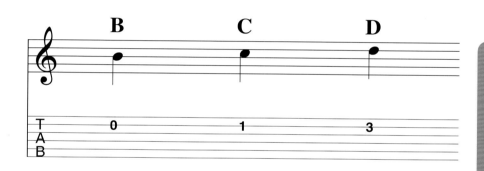

Notes written above the middle line of a staff usually have their stems going down. Notes written below the middle line of the staff usually have their stems going up. The stem for the **B note** can go up or down.

Memorizing Notes

It is important to **memorize** new notes as soon as possible. This way you can concentrate on the timing and sound of the music.

Watching the notation and naming the notes out loud as you play is a good way to memorize notes. Do this with the notes **B**, **C** and **D** several times, as shown in the notation above. Then try playing them with your eyes closed, once again naming the notes out loud.

As you progress through the book, there will be lots of new notes to learn and memorize. The better you know the notes in these early lessons, the easier you will find it to learn higher and lower versions of the notes on other strings.

The Half Note

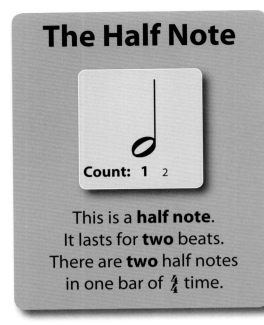

Count: 1 2

This is a **half note**.
It lasts for **two** beats.
There are **two** half notes
in one bar of 4/4 time.

The Half Note Strum

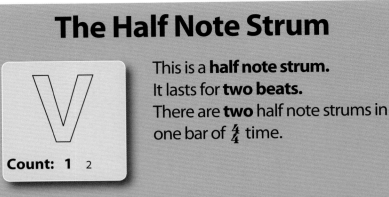

Count: 1 2

This is a **half note strum.**
It lasts for **two beats.**
There are **two** half note strums in
one bar of 4/4 time.

In the count, the larger bold numbers indicate
when a note or strum is played.
The smaller numbers indicate to hold that note
or strum until the next **bold** number.

The following examples use all of the notes and chords you have learnt so far.
The chord symbols and strums have been written above the staff. The melody line (notes) has
been written on the staff. To hear what both parts sound like together, listen to the DVD.
You can practice playing along with either the chords or the notes.

Exercise 10

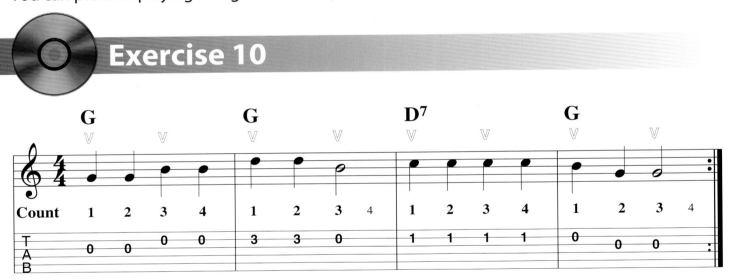

The Importance of Timing

Good timing is one of the most important things a musician needs to develop. To help you
keep time, **count out loud** as you play and **tap your foot** on each beat of the bar, regardless of
whether a quarter note or half note appears in the music. Take it **slowly** at first, and keep your
counting and tapping strong and steady. If you make a mistake when playing, don't stop. Keep
counting and tapping and pick up the next note or chord. Most mistakes are only noticeable if
you draw attention to them.

Exercise 11

Ode to Joy

This song is the melody to **Beethoven's 9th Symphony**. Instead of writing the strumming above each bar of music, it is easier to write it as a **Rhythm Pattern**. This indicates which strumming pattern to use in each bar throughout the song. In bar 8 there are two chords and each one receives two counts. Remember to use the **slide finger** when changing between the **G** and **D7**.

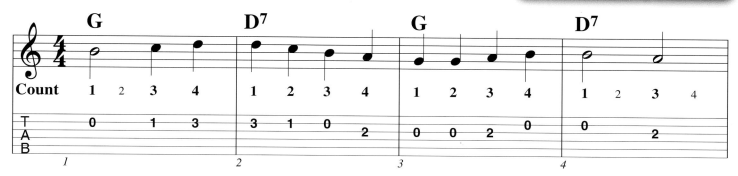

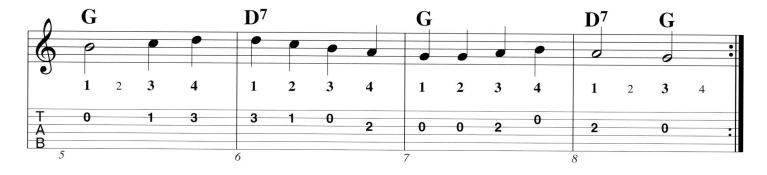

Left Hand Technique

Remember to press down with the **tips of the fingers** to play notes and chords. This produces the clearest sound, and gives you the most control when changing from one finger position to another.

Memorize the melody **Ode to Joy** and watch your left hand as you play it. Make sure you play with the tip of each finger just behind the fret. Listen carefully as you play and aim for a **strong**, **even tone**.

Play very **slowly** until you can do it **perfectly** with control over each finger. Don't worry about playing fast at this stage, speed will come automatically once you can play with control.

Lesson 4

C Major Chord

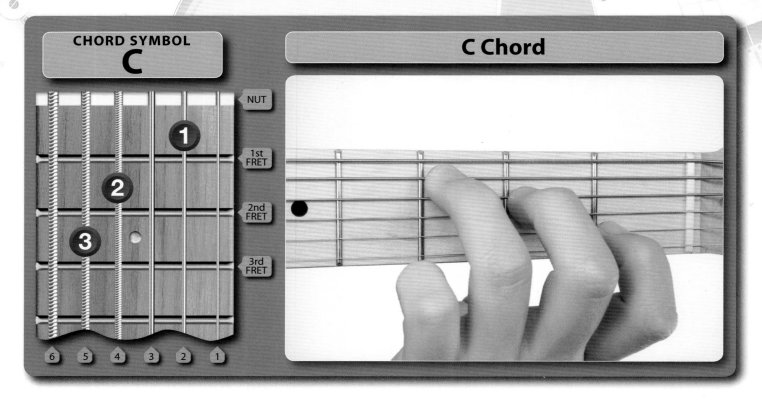

CHORD SYMBOL
C

C Chord

NUT

1st FRET

2nd FRET

3rd FRET

To play the **C** chord, place your **first**, **second** and **third** fingers of your left hand as shown in the diagram. Strum **all six strings**. The red dots indicate the chord has a major tonality.

 ## Exercise 12

The following chord progression contains the three chords you have learnt so far.

Always end a chord progression by strumming the first chord. There are four quarter note strums in each bar (as indicated by the rhythm pattern). Use the **slide finger** when changing between **G** and **D7**.

RHYTHM PATTERN

V	V	V	V
1	2	3	4

G   D⁷   C   D⁷

Count   1   2   3   4   1   2   3   4   1   2   3   4   1   2   3   4

The Pivot

When changing between the **C** and **D7** chords the first finger does not move. The note played by the first finger (a C note) is common to both chords. The second and third fingers move to their new position and the first finger acts as a **pivot**.

G Seventh Chord

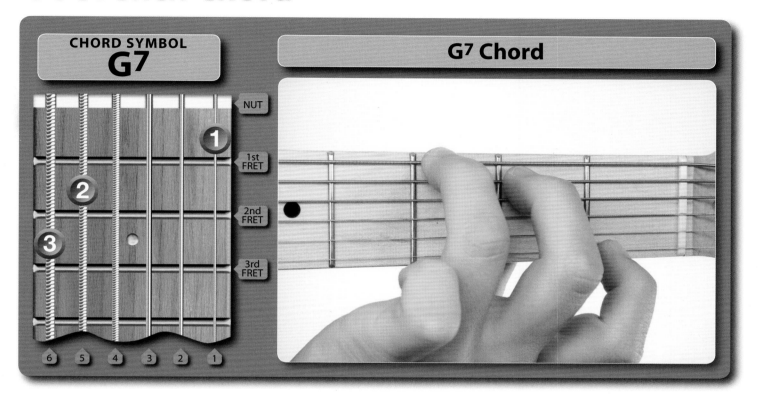

CHORD SYMBOL
G7

G⁷ Chord

NUT

1st FRET

2nd FRET

3rd FRET

6 5 4 3 2 1

To play the **G7** chord, place the **first, second** and **third** fingers of your left hand as shown in the diagram. Strum **all six strings**.

Visualizing Chords

When learning to change between chords, it helps to **visualize** the chord you are about to change to. Try holding a **C** chord shape and picture in your mind where your fingers would move to for a **G7** chord. Then move your fingers and form the **G7** chord.

By visualizing chords, you are giving your fingers very clear information and this will build your confidence and make chord changes easier. It will also make the process of **learning songs** easier, as most sheet music contains chord symbols but doesn't show the shapes. If you can visualise a chord when you see the symbol, you won't have to refer to another book or chord chart every time you learn a new song.

Lesson 5
Common Time Signature

Exercise 13

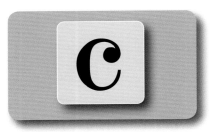

This symbol is called **common time**.
It means exactly the same as $\frac{4}{4}$

RHYTHM PATTERN

V	V	V	V
1	2	3	4

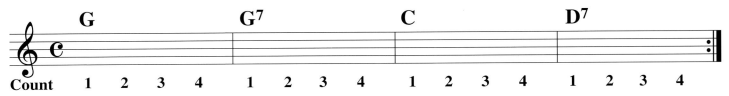

Rests

A **rest** is a period of silence. **Small** count-numbers are placed under rests. If a **rest** comes after you have played a note, you must stop the note sounding. To do this, lift your finger off the fret but keep it lightly touching the string. To stop an open string sounding, lightly touch it with any finger of your left hand.

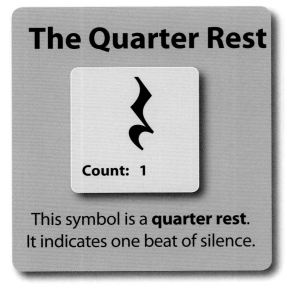

The Quarter Rest

Count: 1

This symbol is a **quarter rest**.
It indicates one beat of silence.

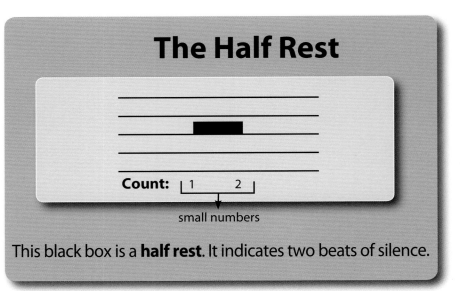

The Half Rest

Count: 1 2

small numbers

This black box is a **half rest**. It indicates two beats of silence.

Rests are just as important as notes. They are like **breathing spaces** in between sentences. If people spoke continuously without pauses and breaths, nobody would be able to understand them. It is the same with music. Rests help the listener absorb the phrase they have just heard. A rest can also help accent or bring attention to the note that follow.

Exercise 14

Aura Lee

This song **Aura Lee** uses all the notes and chords you have learnt so far. It also contains quarter and half rests. Remember to count as you play to help you keep time. It is important to keep counting regardless of whether a note or a rest appears in the music.

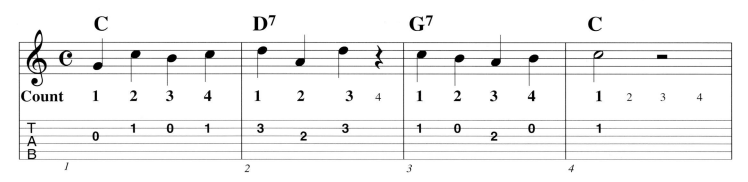

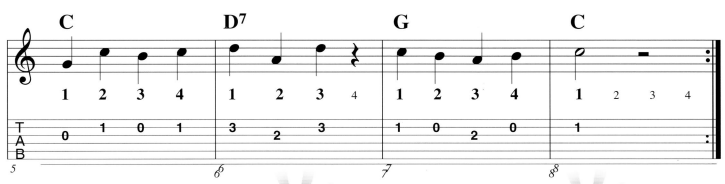

PIVOT
when changing between **C** and **D7** use the first finger as a pivot.

SLIDE FINGER
when changing between **G** and **D7** use the slide finger.

Lesson 6

Notes on the 1st String

The E Note

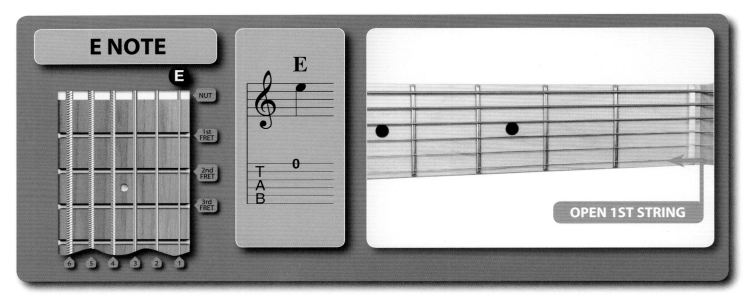

To play the note **E** pick the open **1st string** (no fingers placed behind frets).

The F Note

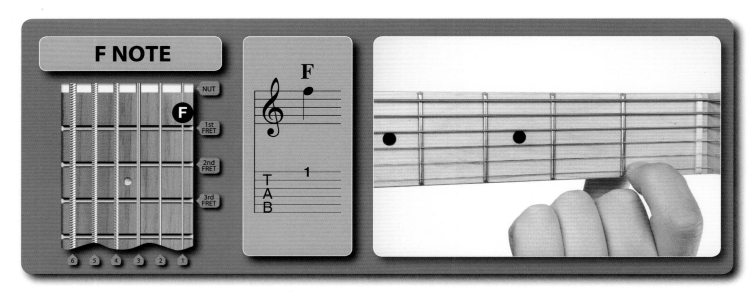

To play the note **F** place the **first finger** of your left hand just behind the **first fret** of the **1st string**.

The G Note

G NOTE

NUT
1st FRET
2nd FRET
3rd FRET

G

6 5 4 3 2 1

To play the note **G** place the **third finger** of your left hand just behind the **third fret** of the **1st string**.

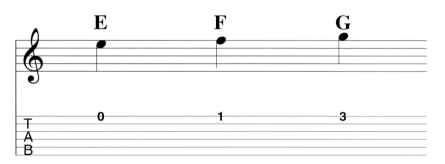

E   F   G

0   1   3

You now know two G notes. The open 3rd string and the third fret of the 1st string. These two G notes are said to be an **octave** apart.

The Whole Note

O

Count: **1** 2 3 4

This is a **whole note**.
It lasts for **four** beats.
There is one whole note
in one bar of $\frac{4}{4}$ time.

The Whole Rest

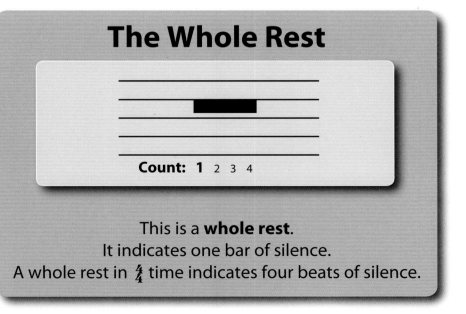

Count: **1** 2 3 4

This is a **whole rest**.
It indicates one bar of silence.
A whole rest in $\frac{4}{4}$ time indicates four beats of silence.

Rock Riff 1

A **Riff** is a pattern of notes that are repeated.
The following example contains a two bar riff played twice.
The example is then repeated and ended by a whole note (G note).

RHYTHM PATTERN

V		V	
1	2	**3**	4

AS A GENERAL RULE: Play notes on the **first** fret with your **first** finger.
Play notes on the **second** fret with your **second** finger.
Play notes on the **third** fret with your **third** finger.

Musical Styles: Rock

Uses both rhythm and lead guitar techniques and sounds. Rock music is mostly in $\frac{4}{4}$ time.
It makes use of both open chords and bar chords, along with scales, riffs and improvised
solos. Rock is usually played on electric guitars.
To learn how to play Rock guitar, see *www.learntoplaymusic.com*

Know your Guitars…

FENDER STRATOCASTER

*The Fender Stratocaster is one of the most famous of all electric guitars.
Designed by Leo Fender and first released in 1954, the Stratocaster
(commonly called a "Strat") has been used by millions of guitarists all
over the world. Some of the most famous Strat players include Jimi
Hendrix, Mark Knopfler and Eric Clapton.*

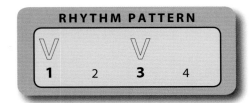

Marianne

Marianne is a Caribbean folk song. It contains a **whole rest** in bars 4, 8, 12 and 16.

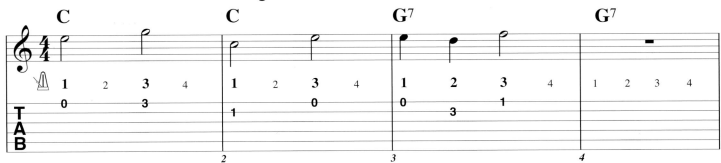

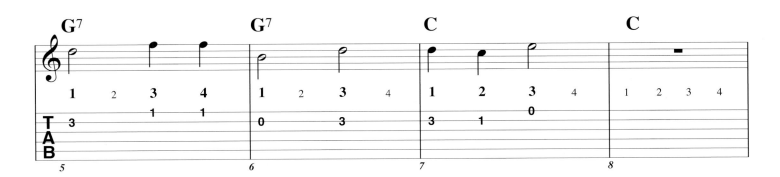

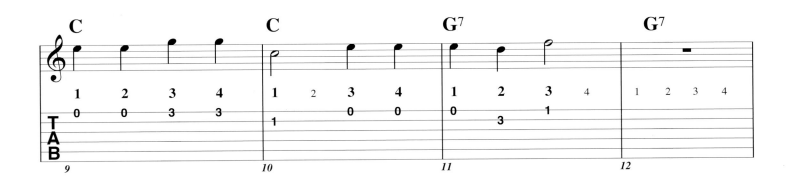

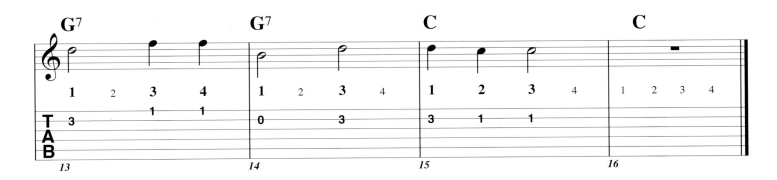

Lesson 7

The Eighth Note

Count: 1

This is an **eighth note**. It lasts for **half a count**. There are **eight** eighth notes in one bar of $\frac{4}{4}$ time.

When eighth notes are joined together the tails are replaced by one **beam**.

BEAM

Count: 1   +

Two eighth notes joined together.

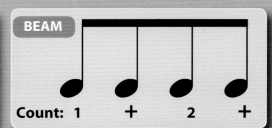

BEAM

Count: 1   +   2   +

Four eighth notes joined together.

Exercise 17

How to Count Eighth Notes

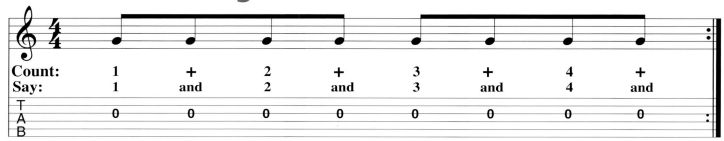

Count:	1	+	2	+	3	+	4	+
Say:	1	and	2	and	3	and	4	and

T A B: 0 0 0 0 0 0 0 0

Alternate Picking

All of the songs you have played so far have involved a downward pick motion, indicated by a V. With the introduction of eighth notes, the technique of down and up ($\wedge$) picking is used. This is called **alternate picking**, and is essential for the development of speed and accuracy.

In alternate picking, use a down pick **on** the beat (the number count) and an up pick **off** the beat (the 'and' count). Do not confuse the pick symbol V (for playing downstrokes) with the strum symbol **V** (for strumming chords).

Exercise 18

Rock Riff 2

Play the following Rock Riff using alternate picking.

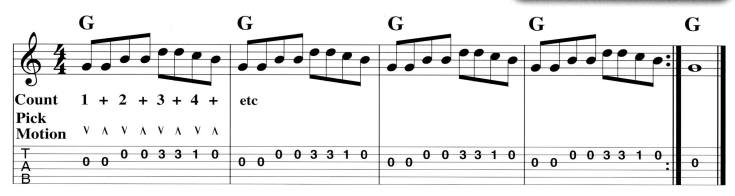

Exercise 19

Hush Little Baby

A traditional children's song which makes use of half notes, quarter notes and eighth notes. Use alternate picking when playing the eighth notes in this song.

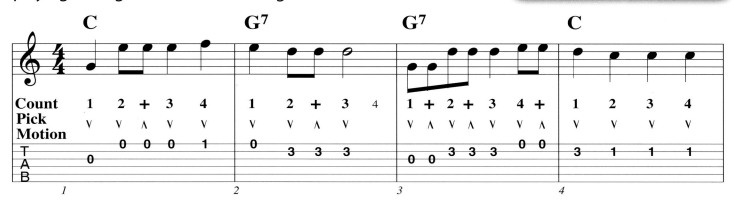

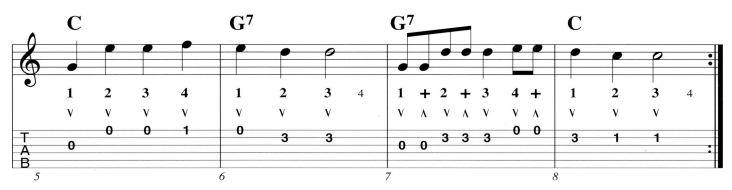

Lesson 8

Eighth Note Rhythms

All the rhythm patterns you have played so far involved playing a downward strum (**V**), on the 1st, 2nd, 3rd or 4th beat.

To make rhythm patterns more interesting, **eighth note rhythm patterns** can be used. An eighth note rhythm is a combination of a down and an up strum within one beat.

The down strum "on the beat" is played louder than the up strum, which is "off the beat" (the "+" section of the count).

An **up strum** is indicated by a **∧** , and is played on the "**and**" section of the count. Start the up strum on the first (thinnest) string and strum all six strings.

Play the following rhythm pattern which has eighth note strums on the second beat, consisting of a down strum on the "2" count and an up strum on the "+" section of the count. There are **eight** eighth note strums in one bar of $\frac{4}{4}$ time

Exercise 20

Eighth Note Rhythm Patterns

Practice this new rhythm pattern holding a **G** chord, then apply it to the chord progression below.

Don't forget to **count and tap your foot** when playing any new rhythm. This will help keep your timing strong and even. Keep the same **tempo** (speed) all the way through, regardless of the chord changes.

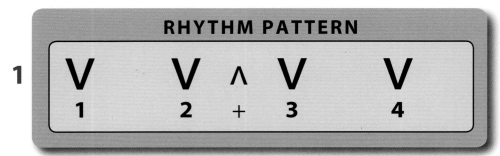

RHYTHM PATTERN

1   V   V ∧ V   V
    1   2 + 3   4

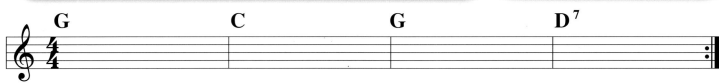

G   C   G   D⁷

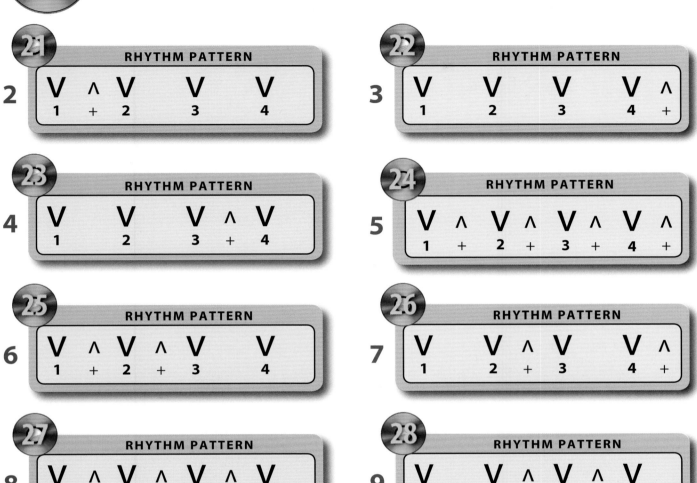

Playing Air

When you play two consecutive down strums, you have to do an up strum in the air to be ready for the second down strum. When playing eighth note rhythms, you can take advantage of this to help you keep a steady rhythm.

Try playing **exercise 24** in the air just above the strings, counting **one and two and three and four and**. This is called **"playing air"**. Repeat the motion while counting four bars of eighth notes. Once you are comfortable doing this, play **exercises 21** to **28**, keeping the up and down motion going the whole time. Simply lower your hand so the pick strikes the strings in the timing indicated in each rhythm pattern.

If you can train yourself to "play air" automatically when playing rhythm guitar, it will help you get into the feeling of the music. When playing along with a recording or playing with a band, you will often find your **right hand** playing the same rhythm as the **drummer's hi-hat pattern**. By locking in with this pattern, you can make the band sound 'tight' and propel the rhythm forward.

Lesson 9

12 Bar Blues

12 Bar Blues is a pattern of chords which repeats every 12 bars.

There are hundreds of well known songs based on this chord progression, i.e. they contain basically the same chords in the same order. 12 bar Blues is commonly used in Rock music and is the basis of Blues music.

Some well known songs which use this 12 bar chord pattern are:

Original Batman TV Theme	Dizzy Miss Lizzy - The Beatles
Hound Dog - Elvis Presley	Red House - Jimi Hendrix
Rock Around the Clock - Bill Hayley	Rock and Roll - Led Zeppelin
Johnny B Goode - Chuck Berry	The Jack - AC/DC
Blue Suede Shoes - Elvis Presley	Give Me One Reason - Tracy Chapman
In the Mood - Glenn Miller	Ice Cream Man - Van Halen
Barbara Ann - The Beach Boys	Blue Jean Blues - ZZ Top

Musical Styles: Blues

Like Rock, Blues uses elements of both rhythm and lead guitar. It contains many bends, slides and other techniques. Blues also makes use of triplets and swing rhythms. It can be played with a pick or fingerstyle. To learn how to play Blues guitar, see *Progressive Complete Learn to Play Blues Guitar Manual*.

Know your Guitars…

GIBSON 335
Many Blues and Jazz players favor hollow body electric guitars for their full, rich tone. One of the most famous hollow body electrics is the Gibson 335. It has been used by players like Freddy King, Magic Sam and Larry Carlton. BB King had a model called the 345 specially designed for him. His guitar is named Lucille.

12 Bar Blues in the Key of G Major

The following 12 bar Blues is in the **key of G major** and uses some of the chords you have learnt so far. When a song is said to be in the key of **G major**, it means that the most important chord (and usually the first chord) is the **G** chord.

This pattern of chords will probably sound familiar to you. Instead of writing a chord symbol above each bar of music, it is common to only write a chord symbol when the chord changes e.g. the first

four bars of this Blues are a **G** chord.

End this 12 bar Blues by playing a **G** chord.

Use alternate picking when playing the notes.

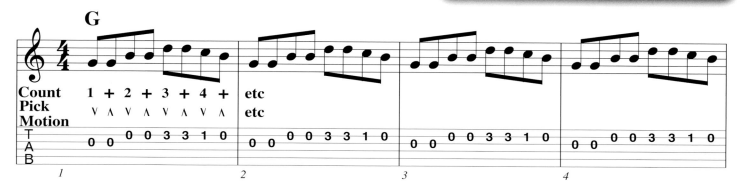

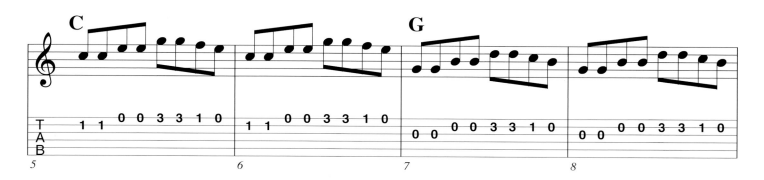

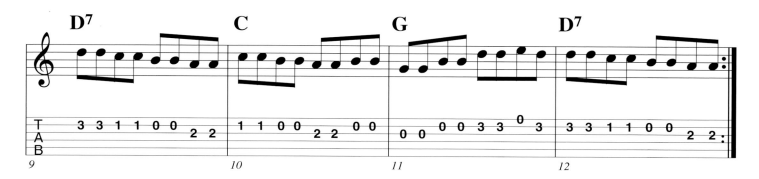

Lesson 10

Notes on the 4th String

The D Note

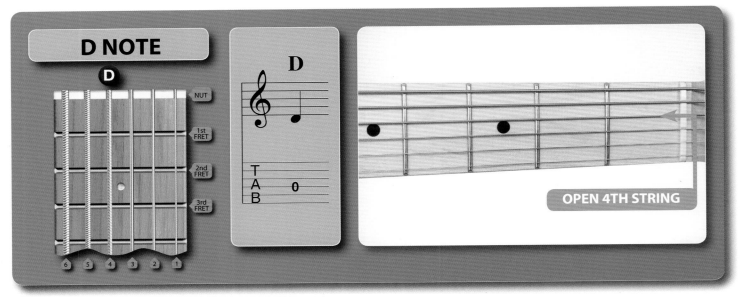

To play the note **D** pick the open **4th string** (no fingers placed behind frets).

The E Note

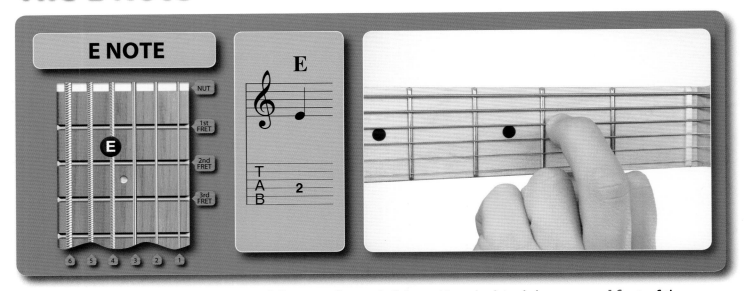

To play the note **E** place the **second finger** of your left hand just behind the **second fret** of the **4th string**.

The F Note

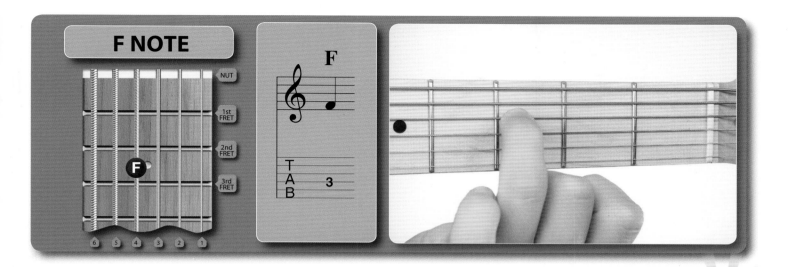

F NOTE

Play the **F** note with the **third finger** of your left hand just behind the **third fret** of the **4th string**.

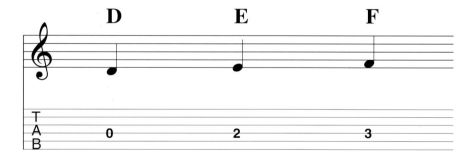

D   E   F

The Notes **D**, **E** and **F** on the 4th string are **one octave lower** than the ones you learned on the 1st and 2nd strings. You now know **two versions** of every note apart from **A** on the 3rd string.

Guitar Effects...
OVERDRIVE
One of the great sounds you can make with an electric guitar and an amp is Overdrive, or Distortion. This is usually achieved with the help of a pedal which you plug into on the way to the amp. The one shown here is an Ibanez Tube Screamer. There are many distortion pedals available with names like Metal Zone, Super Distortion and Fuzz Box. Try some out at a music store.

Minor Chords

There are three main types of chords: **Major**, **Seventh** and **Minor.**
 The chord symbol for the minor chord is a small '**m**' placed after the letter name.

D Minor Chord

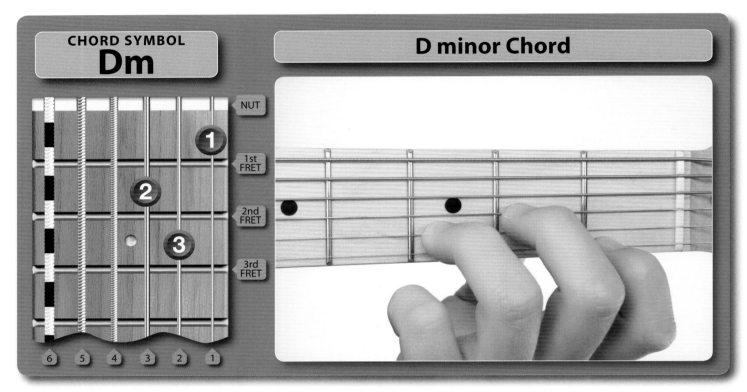

Purple colored dots indicate the chord has a minor tonality.

 ## Exercise 30

To play the **Dm** chord, use the **first**, **second** and **third** fingers of your left hand as shown in the diagram. Strum only **five** strings.

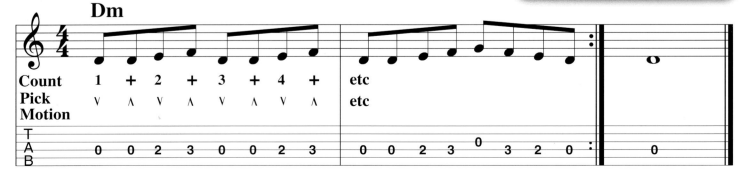

Exercise 31

The following example contains a **D minor** chord and uses notes on the 4th string.

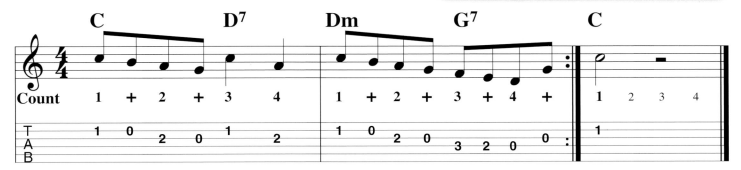

Use your **first** finger as a pivot when changing between **C** and **D7**.
Use your **second** finger as a pivot when changing between **D7** and **Dm**.
Use your **first** finger as a pivot when changing between **Dm** and **G7**.

The use of pivot fingers will make chord changes easier. This also applies to slide fingers. Both of these techniques will also make your chord changes sound smoother.

Look for the possibility of using these techniques when changing between any two chords. Try to make them an automatic, instinctive part of your playing. It is important to do this with every new technique you learn, as the more techniques you have at your disposal, the easier you will find it to learn new songs.

Know your Guitars…
ACOUSTIC CUTAWAY
As well as the standard acoustic guitar, there is another version called a Cutaway where part of the body of the guitar is cut back and reshaped along the side of the fretboard. This makes it easier to play notes high up on the fretboard, which is great for playing Lead solos on an acoustic guitar. Many players who switch frequently between acoustic and electric prefer to use an acoustic cutaway.

Lesson 11
Turnaround Progressions

In **lesson 9**, you were introduced to the 12 Bar Blues chord progression. Another common chord progression to learn is called the **Turnaround**. Like 12 Bar Blues, it is the basis of many songs, and it will probably sound familiar to you. Unlike 12 Bar Blues, where the progression occurs over a fixed number of bars, the Turnaround progression may vary in length as in the examples below, however the chord sequence remains the same. Some of the biggest hit songs of all time are based upon the turnaround progression. Every year since the beginning of Rock music there are hit songs based upon 12 Bar Blues and Turnaround progressions.

Stand by Me - John Lennon
Return to Sender - Elvis Presley
All I Have To Do Is Dream - Everly Brothers
Blue Moon - Various Artists
Everlasting Love - U2

Please Mr Postman - The Beatles
Crocodile Rock (chorus) - Elton John
Uptown Girl - Billy Joel
Houses of the Holy - Led Zeppelin
Hungry Heart - Bruce Springsteen

E Minor Chord

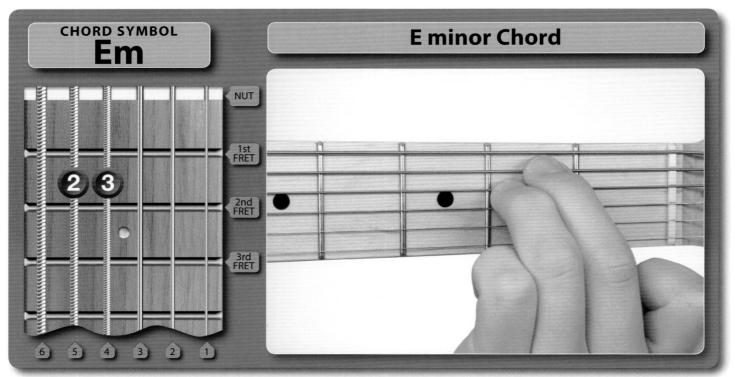

CHORD SYMBOL
Em

E minor Chord

To play the **Em** chord, use the **second** and **third** fingers of your left hand as shown in the diagram. Strum all **six** strings.

www.learntoplaymusic.com

Exercise 32

Turnaround in the Key of G Major

All Turnaround progressions contain at least one minor chord. The following chord progression is a turnaround in the **key of G** and it contains a new chord, **E minor (Em)**.

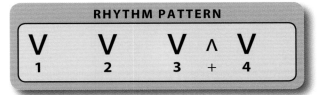

| G | Em | C | D⁷ |

Exercise 33

Turnaround in the Key of G Major

In this Turnaround there are two bars of each chord.

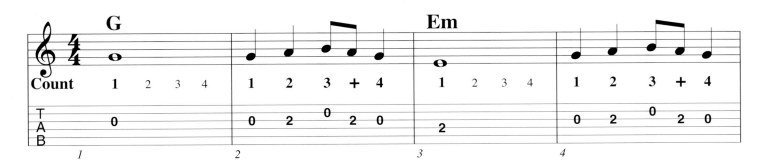

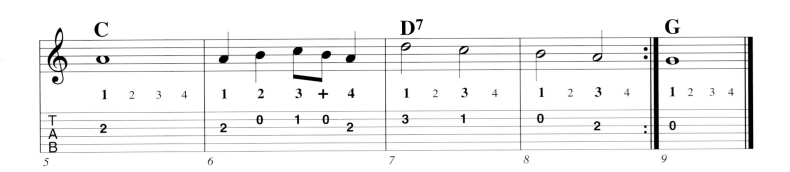

A Minor Chord

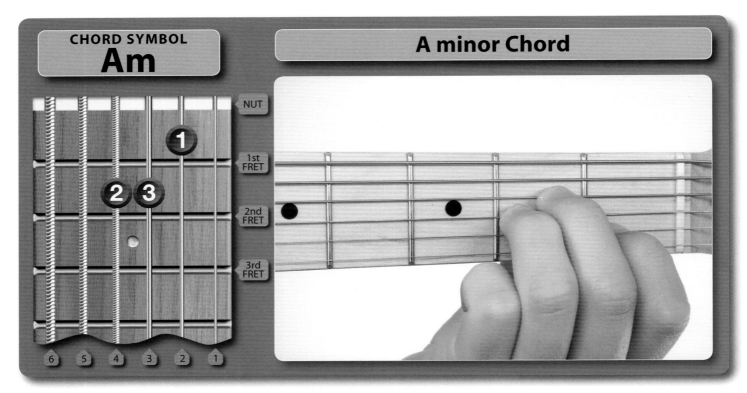

CHORD SYMBOL
Am

A minor Chord

NUT
1st FRET
2nd FRET
3rd FRET

6 5 4 3 2 1

To play the **Am** chord, use the **first**, **second** and **third** fingers of your left hand as shown in the diagram. Strum all **six** strings.

Revision of Chords

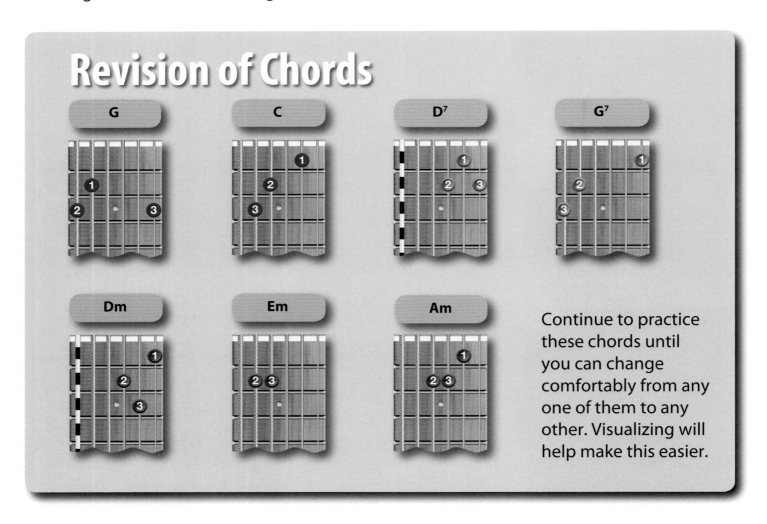

G   C   D⁷   G⁷

Dm   Em   Am

Continue to practice these chords until you can change comfortably from any one of them to any other. Visualizing will help make this easier.

Turnaround in the Key of C Major

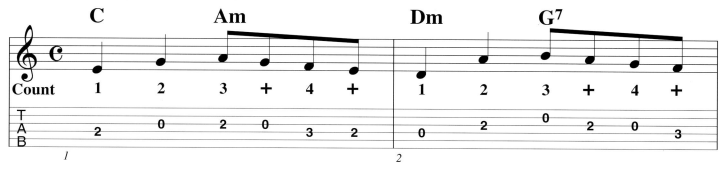

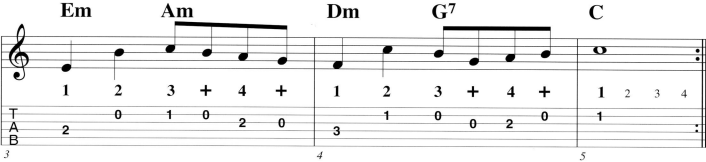

Notice that the chord progression of this example sounds similar to the previous Turnaround in the key of G. It is useful to be able to play Turnaround progressions in several different keys, as this will mean you already know the chords for many different songs.

Accessories...

THE CAPO

The Capo is a device which is placed across the neck of the guitar (acting as a moveable nut). This enables you to change the key of a song without changing the chord shapes. It also allows you to play easier chord shapes for songs in difficult keys. To learn how to use a Capo, see Progressive Complete Learn to Play Rhythm Guitar Manual or Progressive Complete Learn to Play Fingerpicking Guitar Manual.

Lesson 12

Notes on the 5th String

The A Note

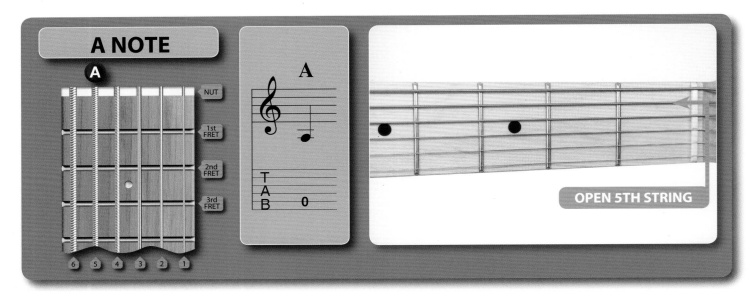

To play the note **A** pick the open **5th string** (no fingers placed behind frets).

The B Note

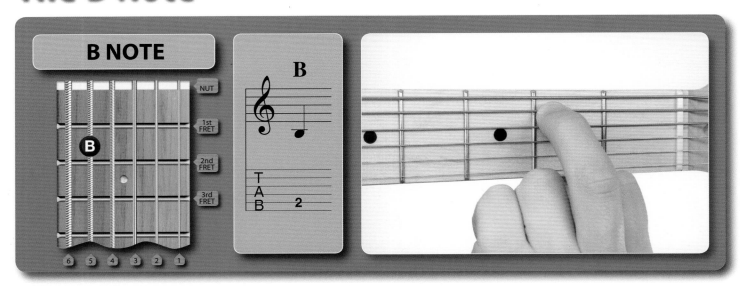

To play the note **B** place the **second finger** of your left hand just behind the **second fret** of the **5th string.**

The C Note

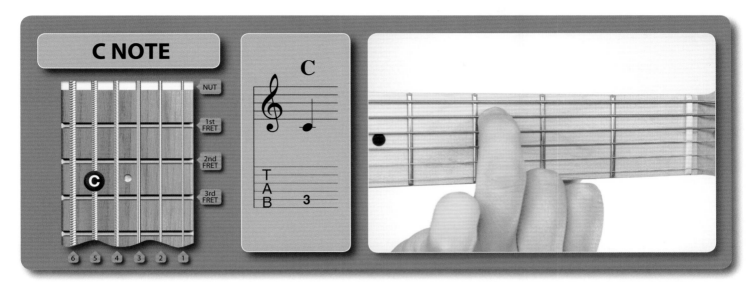

Play the **C** note with the **third finger** of your left hand just behind the **third fret** of the **5th string**.

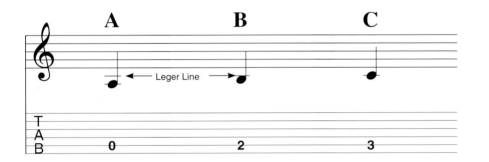

LEGER LINE
A short line placed beneath the staff is called a **Leger Line**.

Practice changing between **A**, **B** and **C** while watching your left hand. Make sure you play on the tips of the fingers and name the notes out loud. When you can do this easily, play them with your eyes closed, while visualising the notes in your mind. This will prepare you for playing the new notes while reading the music.

Know your Guitars...

GIBSON LES PAUL

Along with the Fender Stratocaster, the Gibson Les Paul is one of the most famous of all Electric guitars. It is great for heavy Rock sounds as well as as being versatile enough for Blues and Jazz. This guitar was made specially for Les Paul - a great Jazz player who also invented multitrack recording. This technique is essential for recording and is now used by everyone from top recording studios to musicians using computers at home.

E Seventh Chord

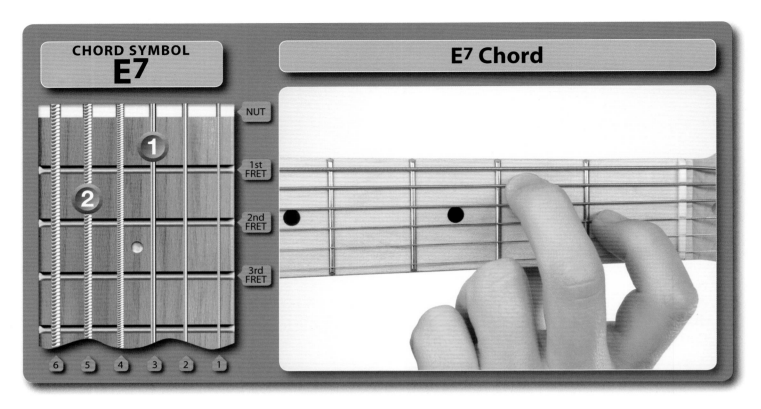

CHORD SYMBOL
E7

E⁷ Chord

To play the **E7** chord, use the **first** and **second** fingers of your left hand as shown in the diagram. Strum all **six** strings.

Exercise 35

Melody in the Key of A minor

Songs can also be in a minor key.
This melody is in the **key of A minor**.

RHYTHM PATTERN

V		V	∧	V		V
1		**2**	**+**	**3**		**4**

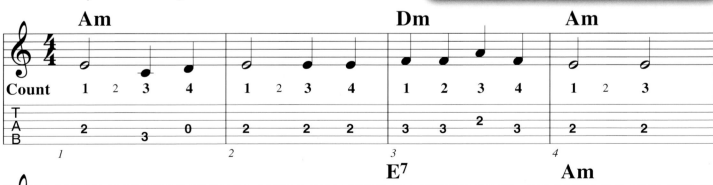

F Major Chord

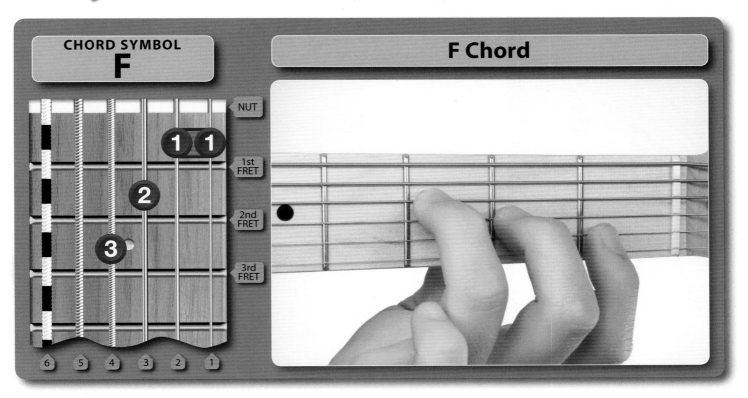

CHORD SYMBOL
F

F Chord

6 5 4 3 2 1

To play the **F** chord, use the **first**, **second** and **third** fingers of your left hand as shown in the diagram. Strum only **five** strings. The first finger bars across the first two strings. This is quite difficult at first. The **F** chord is easier to play if you position your **third** and **second** fingers before you position the **first** finger.

As with previous chords, it will help if you can visualise exactly where your fingers will go before you move them to form the **F** chord.

 ## Exercise 36

Turnaround in the Key of C

The following chord progression is a Turnaround in the key of **C**. When changing between **Am** and **F**, release the pressure on the **first** finger but do not lose contact with the string as you bar the 1st and 2nd strings. When changing between **C** and **Am**, only the **third** finger moves.

RHYTHM PATTERN

V   V
1   2   3   4

C   Am   F   G⁷

Lesson 13

The Dotted Quarter Note

Count: 1

A dot written after a quarter note means that you hold the note for **one and a half** beats.

Count: 1   2   +

A dotted quarter note is often followed by an eighth note.

Exercise 37

Turnaround in C Major

Here is a melody based on a turnaround in C which features the use of dotted quarter notes.

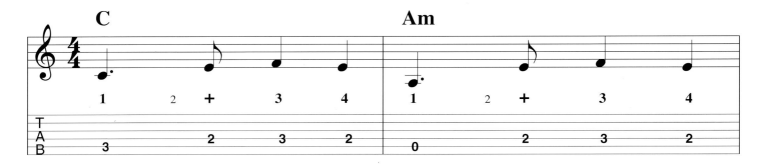

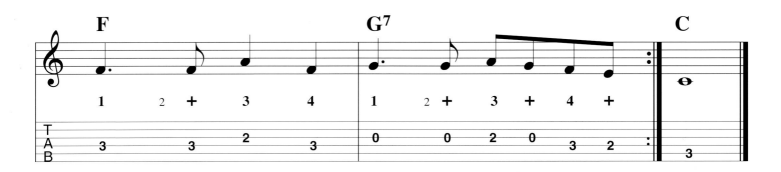

Notes on the 6th String

The E Note

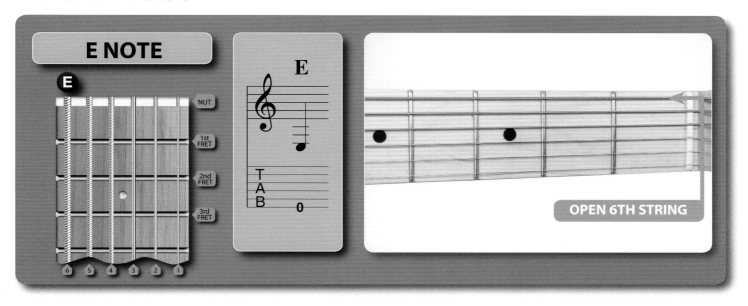

To play the note **E** pick the open **6th string** (no fingers placed behind frets).

The F Note

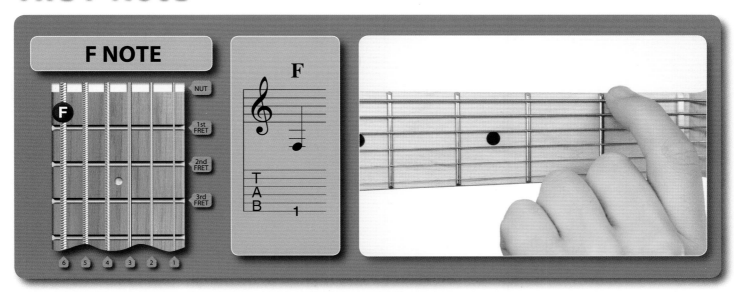

To play the note **F** place the **first finger** of your left hand just behind the **first fret** of the **6th string**.

The G Note

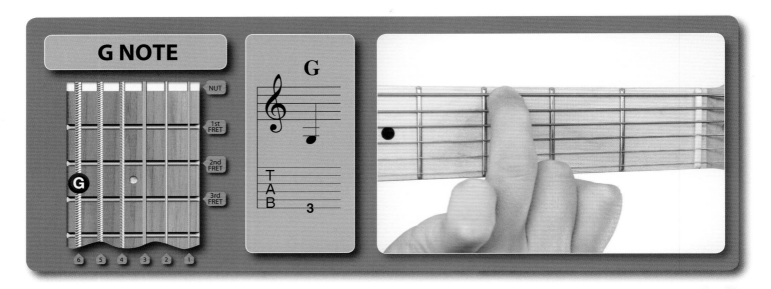

G NOTE

To play the note **G** place the **third finger** of your left hand just behind the **third fret** of the **6th string**.

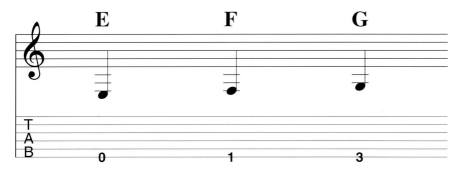

E   F   G

T		
A		
B	0	1	3

These E, F and G notes are an octave below the ones on the 4th and 3rd strings. You now know 3 versions of these notes.

Revision of Notes

Here is a summary of all the notes you have learnt so far.
Run through them both ascending and descending while reading the diagram, and say the names of the notes out loud as you play. Then run through them again with your eyes closed, still naming the notes out loud. This will help consolidate the notes in your memory.

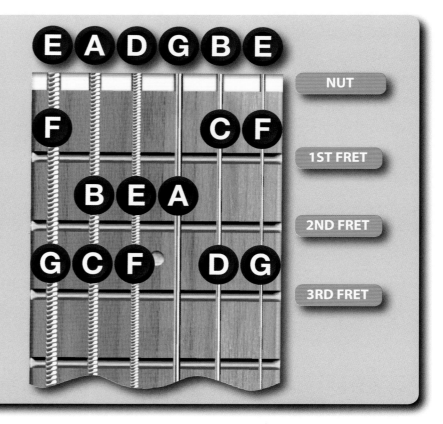

Exercise 38

Melody in the Key of E minor

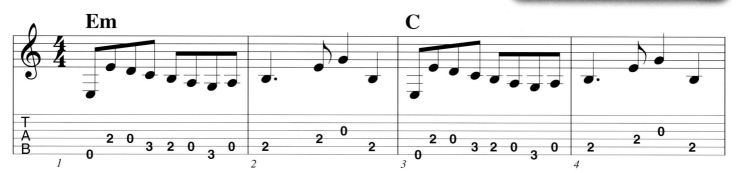

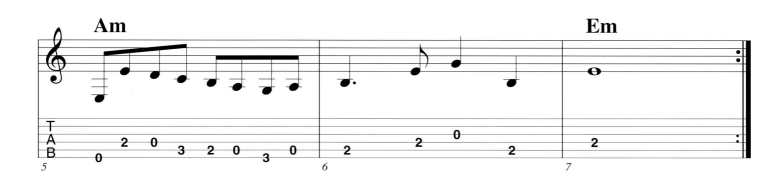

Notice that melodies in a minor key have a different type of sound to those in major keys. **Minor keys** are often described as having a **sadder** sound than major keys.

Guitar Effects...

THE CHORUS PEDAL

The Chorus pedal is an ambient effect which creates a feeling of space and movement within the sound. The pedal delays the sound and changes it to become less regular and also adds slight pitch fluctuations. It then mixes this version of the sound in with the original signal coming from the guitar. Chorus pedals are equally effective with both acoustic and electric guitars.

Lesson 14

The Lead-In

Sometimes a song does not begin on the first beat of the bar. Any notes which come before the first full bar are called **lead-in notes** (or **pick-up notes**). When lead-in notes are used, the last bar is also incomplete. The notes in the lead-in and the notes in the last bar add up to one full bar. When you are playing chords do not strum until the first full bar, after the lead-in notes.

First and Second Endings

The next song contains **first and second endings**. The first time you play through the song, play the first ending, (⌐1.⌐), then go back to the beginning. The second time you play through the song, play the second ending, (⌐2.⌐), instead of the first.

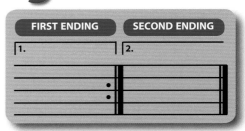

Exercise 39

Mussi Den

Play the first ten bars, then repeat from the beginning but don't play bars 9 and 10 again, instead go to bar 11. Then play to the end of the song. A half rest is in bar 10. The half rest and the two lead-in notes at the beginning of the song add up to one complete bar (i.e. 4 beats). This song is in the key of **C major**.

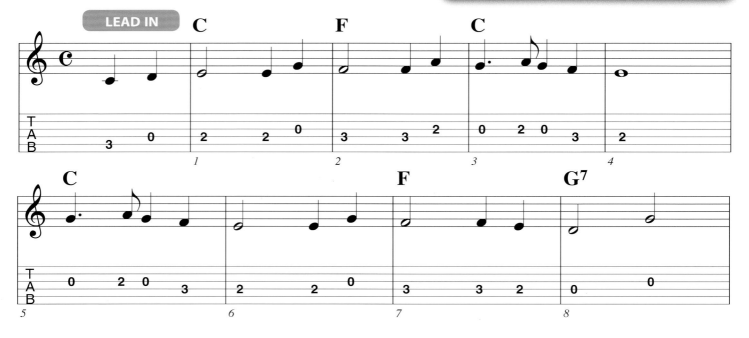

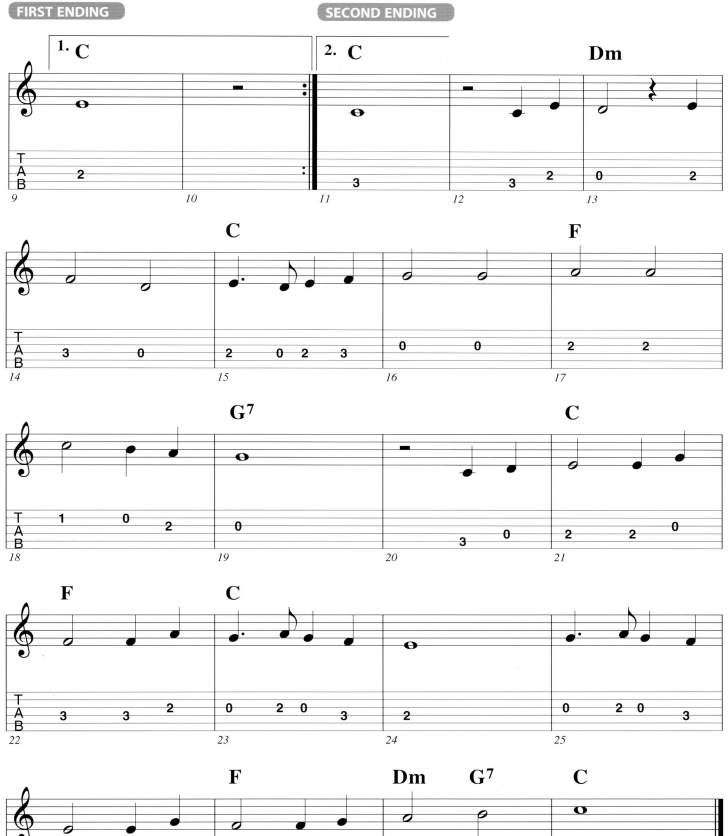

Lesson 15

The Major Scale

The **major scale** is a series of **8** notes in alphabetical order that has the familiar sound:

| Do | Re | Mi | Fa | So | La | Ti | Do |

The **C major scale** contains the following notes.

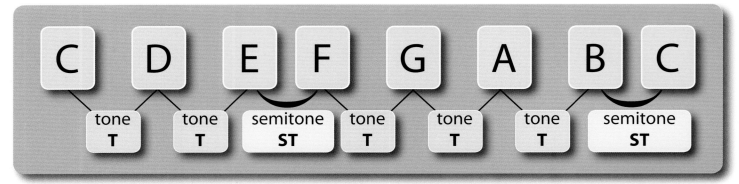

The distance between each note is two frets, except for **E F** and **B C** where the distance is only one fret. The distance of two frets is called a **tone**, indicated by **T**. The distance of one fret is called a **semitone**, indicated by **ST**.

The major scale is the most commonly used grouping of notes in music. It has been used to create thousands of melodies in many different styles of music. This includes Rock songs, Folk songs, Jazz guitar lines and even themes of Classical symphonies. The major scale is also essential for creating harmonies and constructing chords.

The Octave

An **octave** is the range of **8 notes** of a scale.
The first note and last note of a scale always have the same name.
In the **C major** scale the distance from the lowest C to the C note above it is one octave (8 notes). The following example is one octave of the C major scale.

The C Major Scale

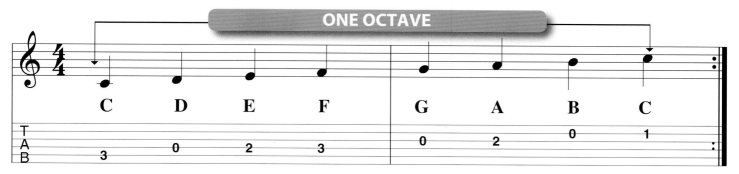

Each of the 8 notes in the major scale is given a **scale number**.

T = Tone (2 frets)   **ST** = Semitone (1 fret)

The distance between two notes is called an **interval**. In any major scale, the interval between the 3rd to 4th note and the 7th to 8th note is one semitone (1 fret). All other notes are one tone (2 frets) apart.

The Key of C Major

When a song consists of notes from a particular scale, it is said to be written in the **key** which has the same notes as that scale. For example, if a song contains mostly notes from the **C major scale**, it is said to be in the **key of C major**. The songs **"Silent Night"** and **"Morning Has Broken"** are in the key of **C major**.

The Three Four Time Signature

This time signature is called the **three four time signature**. It indicates there are **three** beats in each bar. Three four time is also known as Waltz time. There are three quarter notes in one bar of $\frac{3}{4}$ time.

The Dotted Half Note

Count: **1** 2 3

A dot placed after a note or strum extends its value by **half**. A dot placed after a half note or half note strum means that you hold it for three beats. One dotted half note makes one bar of music in $\frac{3}{4}$ time. There is one dotted half note strum in one bar of music in $\frac{3}{4}$ time.

The Dotted Half Strum

Count: **1** 2 3

Know your Guitars...

The Fender Telecaster

This classic solid body electric guitar is used extensively in Country music and is also popular with Rock, Pop, Soul, Funk and Blues players. It is capable of producing a variety of sounds from clear bell like tones to stinging attacking sounds. Equally effective for both Rhythm and Lead guitar, the Telecaster has been favored by players like James Burton (who played with Elvis Presley), Muddy Waters, Albert Lee and Roy Buchanan.

  www.learntoplaymusic.com

Exercise 41

Silent Night

Silent Night was written by **Franz Gruber**, and it is one of the most popular Christmas songs. It is in $\frac{3}{4}$ time in the key of **C major**. The rhythm pattern contains three beats but only one dotted half strum in $\frac{3}{4}$ time.

Bar 24 contains a whole rest which can also be used in $\frac{3}{4}$ time.

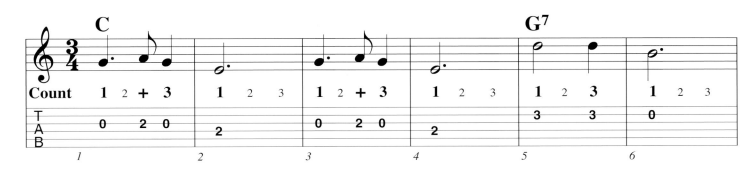

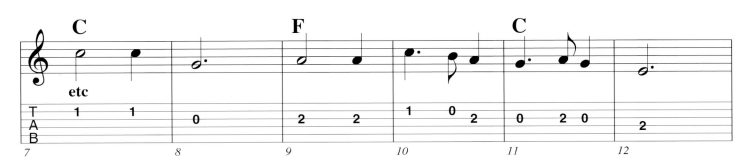

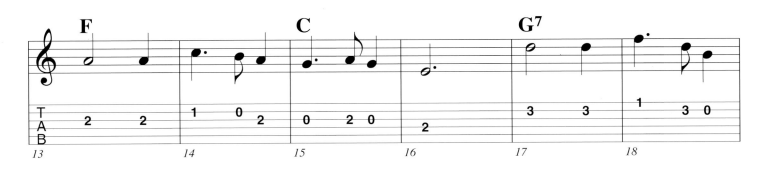

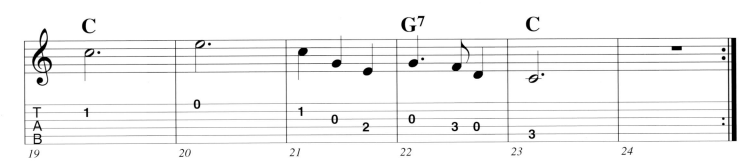

Lesson 17

The Tie

A **tie** is a curved line that connects two notes with the **same** position on the staff.
A tie tells you to pick the **first** note only, and to hold it for the length of both notes.

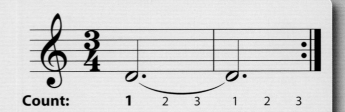

Count: 1 2 3 1 2 3

Pick the D note and hold it for six counts

A tie is the only way of indicating that a note is to be held across a bar line. It is important to remember that tied notes are meant to keep sustaining for the full length of both notes. Do not lift your finger or play the next note until you have counted to the end of the tied notes. On some occasions several notes may be tied rather than just two.

Exercise 42

Morning Has Broken

Morning Has Broken is a well known folk song.
Do not strum any chord for the first bar.
This song is in $\frac{3}{4}$ time and is in the key of **C major**. A **tie** is used to connect the two dotted half notes in bars 11 and 12, and the last two bars.
Once again, rhythm patterns in $\frac{3}{4}$ time contain three beats.

RHYTHM PATTERN

V V ∧ V
1 2 + 3

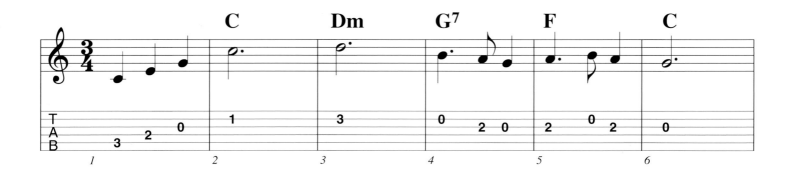

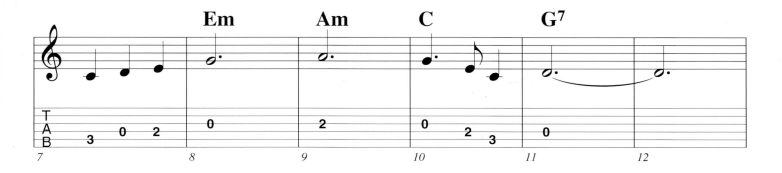

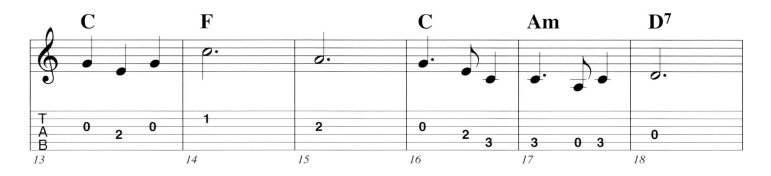

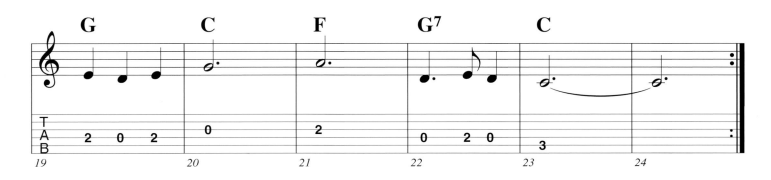

Electric Guitar Pickups...

SINGLE COIL PICKUPS

Electric guitars contain Pickups which capture the sound coming from the strings and send the signal to the amplifier. The original pickups were Single Coil pickups similar to the one shown here. These pickups are commonly found in Fender guitars like the Stratocaster which contains three single coil pickups, and the Telecaster which contains two different single coil pickups.

Lesson 18

The Eighth Note Triplet

Eighth note **triplets** are a group of **three** evenly spaced notes played within one beat. Eighth note triplets are indicated by three eighth notes grouped together by a bracket (or a curved line) and the number **3** written either above or below the group. The eighth note triplets are played with a third of a beat each. **Accent** (play louder) the first note of each triplet group as it will help you keep time.

Count: 1   +   a
Say: **one and ah**

Triplets occur in all styles of music, but they are particularly common in Jazz, Blues and Gospel. Swing and shuffle rhythms, fundamental to modern music are also derived from Triplets. To learn about these rhythms, see *Progressive Complete Learn to Play Lead Guitar Manual.*

 ## Exercise 43

Amazing Grace

Amazing Grace is a Gospel song which has featured in many motion pictures.
It is in $\frac{3}{4}$ time in the key of **G major**.
It has a lead-in and contains eighth note triplets.

RHYTHM PATTERN

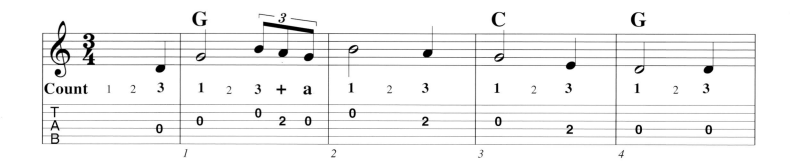

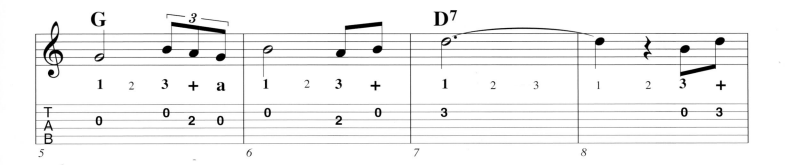

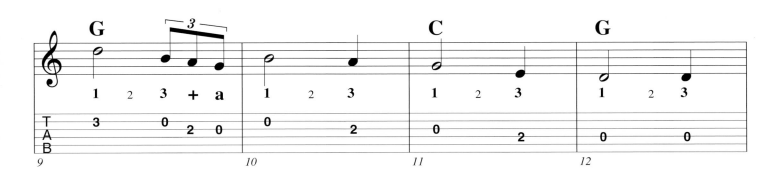

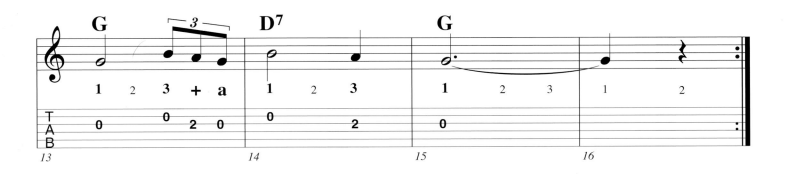

Electric Guitar Pickups...
HUMBUCKERS
Although single coil pickups make a great sound, they can also produce unwanted noise known as hum. In the 1950's, guitar makers discovered that if you put two single coil pickups together, the second one cancels the hum, as well as producing a fatter, warmer sound. Thus the humbucking pickup (Humbucker) was born. These pickups are traditionally associated with Gibson guitars such as the Les Paul and the 335.

Lesson 19

Sharp Signs

This is a **sharp** sign.
A sharp sign written before a note on the staff means that you play the note that is **one fret higher** than the written note.

Written below are two **F sharp** (F#) notes.
When a sharp sign is written on the staff it is always written **before** the note.

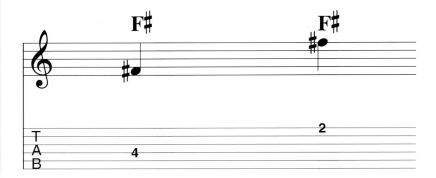

F Sharp Notes

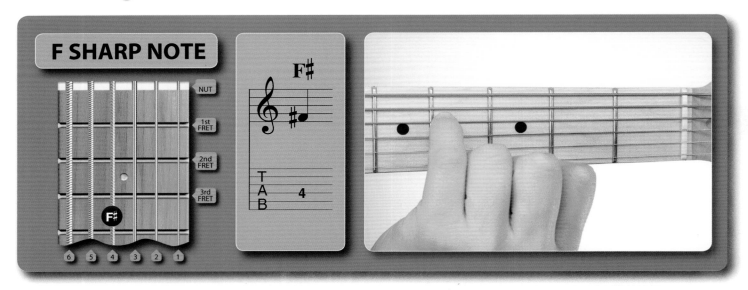

To play this F# note place the **fourth finger** of your left hand just behind the **fourth fret** of the **4th string**.

This is the first note requiring the use of the 4th finger of the left hand. Make sure you press down with the tip of the finger and listen carefully as you pick the string. Aim for a full, clear sound without the string buzzing. Then try playing the notes D, E and F# on the 4th string several times, both ascending and descending.

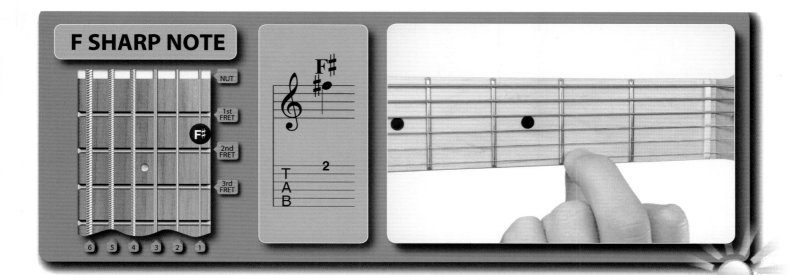

F SHARP NOTE

To play this **F♯** note place the **second finger** of your left hand just behind the **second fret** of the **1st string**.

Notice that the **G major** scale has the same patterns of tones and semitones as the **C major** scale.

The G Major Scale

The **G major** scale starts and ends on the note G and contains an F sharp (**F♯**) note. Written below are two octaves of the **G major** scale. In a major scale, the intervals between the 3rd to 4th note and the 7th to 8th notes are semitones (1 fret). In the **G major** scale, to keep this pattern of tones and semitones correct, an **F♯** note must be used instead of an **F** note.

Exercise 44

The G Major Scale over 2 Octaves

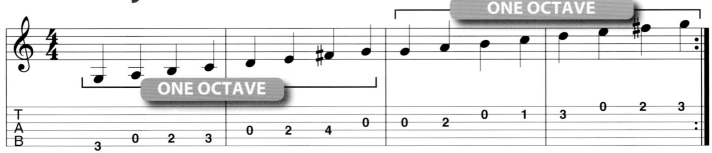

Note	G	A	B	C	D	E	F♯	G	G	A	B	C	D	E	F♯	G
Number	1	2	3	4	5	6	7	8 or	1	2	3	4	5	6	7	8
Pattern		T	T	ST	T	T	T	ST		T	T	ST	T	T	T	ST

Play this F♯ note with the **fourth** finger of your **left** hand.

Play this F♯ note with the **second** finger of your **left** hand.

www.learntoplaymusic.com

BEGINNER BASICS **GUITAR**   PAGE 75

Lesson 20

Key Signatures

The key of **C major** was discussed in lesson **15**. Songs that use notes from the **C major** scale are said to be in the key of **C**. Similarly, songs that use notes from the **G major** scale are said to be in the key of **G major**.

Songs in the key of **G** will contain **F sharp (F♯)** notes. Instead of writing a sharp sign before every F note on the staff, it is easier to write just one sharp sign after each clef. This means that all the F notes on the staff are played as **F♯** even though there is no sharp sign written before them.

This is called a **key signature**. Tab notation does not use a key signature.

C Major Key Signature

The **C major** scale contains no sharps or flats, therefore the key signature for the key of **C major** contains no sharps or flats.

G Major Key Signature

The **G major** scale contains one sharp, F♯, therefore the key signature for the key of **G major** contains one sharp, F♯.

In any particular key, certain chords are more common than others, and after a while you will become familiar with the chords that belong to each key. Certain keys are easier for guitarists to play in and you should learn how to **transpose**, so you can change a song that is in a difficult key (i.e. difficult chord shapes for a beginner) into an easy key.

The easiest keys for a guitarist to play in are the keys of **C major**, **G major**, **A minor** and **E minor**. All of the songs in this book are in these keys.

For every key signature there are two possible keys - one major and one minor. These are known as **Relative Keys**. The keys of C major and A minor are relative keys, as they contain no sharps or flats. The Keys of G major and E minor are relative, both contain one sharp.

www.learntoplaymusic.com

The most common chords in the key of **C major** are – **C**, **Dm**, **Em**, **F**, **G7**, **Am**

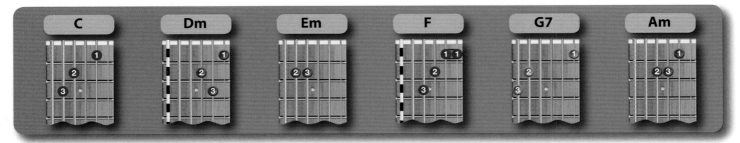

The most common chords in the key of **G major** are – **G**, **Am**, **Bm**, **C**, **D7**, **Em**

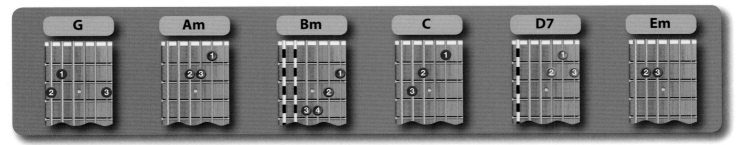

Bass Note Rhythm Patterns

Exercise 45

Bass Note Rhythm Pattern 1

Instead of strumming the complete chord for every beat, try picking the bass note of the chord on the first beat and then strum the first three strings of the chord on the 2nd, 3rd and 4th beats. Play the following **bass note** rhythm pattern holding a **G** chord shape.

Exercise 46

Bass Note Rhythm Pattern 2

A variation to this bass note rhythm pattern is to play the bass note on the first and third beats and strum on the second and fourth beats. Play the following **bass note** rhythm pattern, also holding a **G** chord shape.

The best bass note to pick is the lowest note of the chord that has the same letter name of the chord. This is called the **root note**.

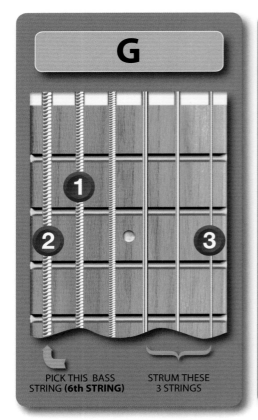

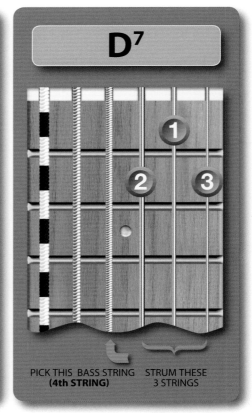

When playing a **G** chord, pick the **6th** string note (**G note**).

When playing a **C** chord, pick the **5th** string note (**C note**).

When playing a **D7** chord, pick the **4th** string note (**D note**).

Practice this rhythm technique on each chord separately at first, and remember to hold the full chord shape even though you are not playing all the strings.

Exercise 47

The song **Waltzing Matilda** is in the **key of G** and contains the three chords shown above. Play the chords using bass note rhythm pattern 2. For the chords that last for a full bar you could also alternate the bass notes. E.g. for the **G** chord play the 6th string bass note on the first beat and play the 4th string bass note on the third beat.

Waltzing Matilda is the most popular and well known Australian folk song. It is in ⁴⁄₄ time in the key of **G major**. Remember, the key signature indicates that all F notes on the staff are played as F♯. Practice this song using the suggested bass note rhythm pattern. There is always more than one rhythm that can be used to accompany a song.

Play the F♯ note on the **4th** string with your **fourth** finger and play the F♯ note on the **1st** string with your **second** finger.

Waltzing Matilda

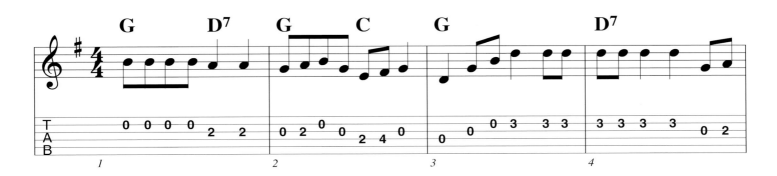

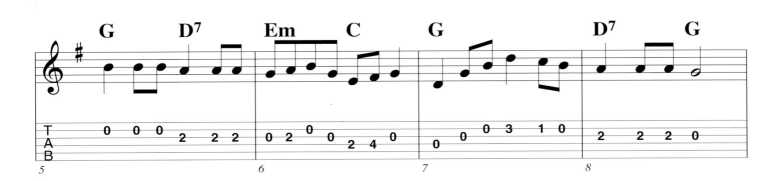

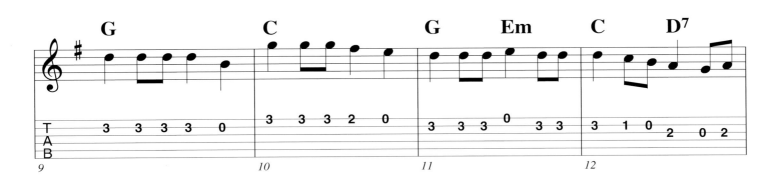

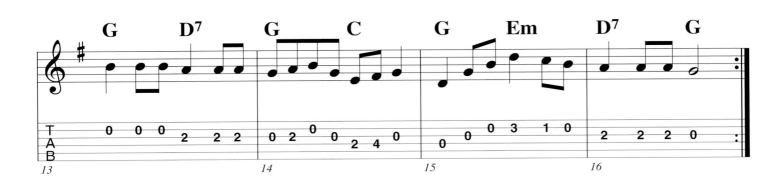

Lesson 21

B Minor Chord

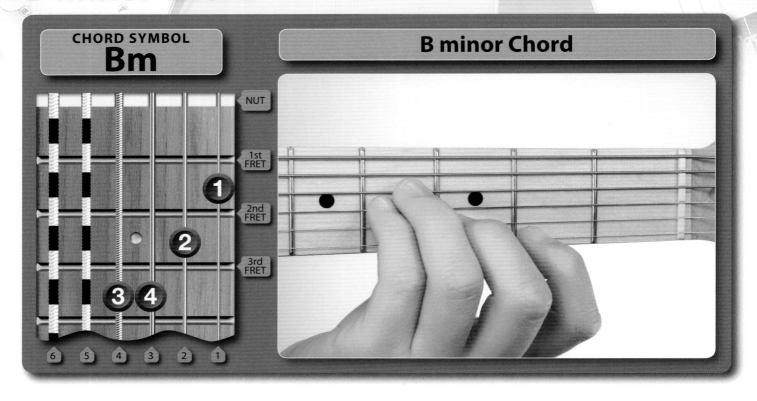

CHORD SYMBOL
Bm

NUT

1st FRET

2nd FRET

3rd FRET

1 **2** **3** **4**

6 5 4 3 2 1

B minor Chord

To play the **Bm** chord, use the **first**, **second**, **third** and **fourth** fingers of your left hand as shown in the diagram. Strum only **four** strings.

Know your Guitars…

The Classical Guitar

The classical guitar has nylon strings and is played with the fingers of the right hand rather than a pick. As the name suggests, this is the type of guitar used for Classical music, but it is also commonly used for Flamenco, Folk, and World music. Some of the most famous Classical guitarists are Andres Segovia, John Williams and Alirio Diaz. American fingerpicker Chet Atkins used an electric Classical guitar.

Exercise 48

Minuet

This song is based upon a minuet by famous classical composer **Bach**. It is in the key of **G major** and contains the **B minor** chord. Notice the key signature and remember to play **F♯** notes instead of F.

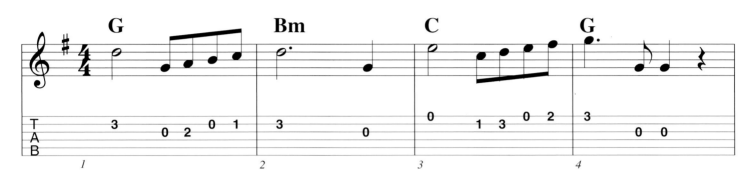

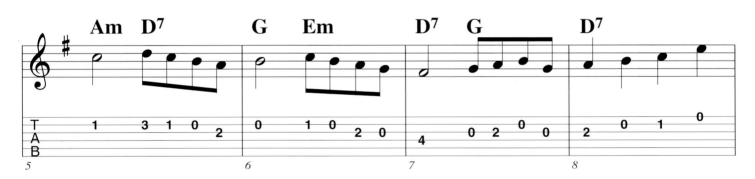

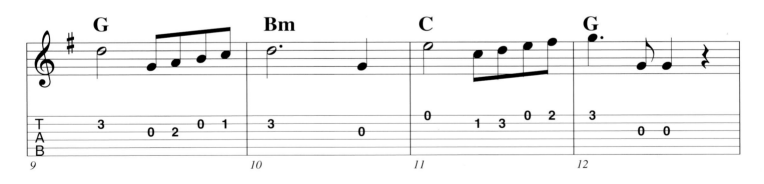

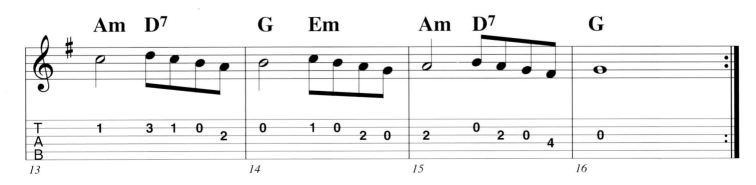

Silent Strums and Continuous Rhythms

RHYTHM PATTERN

V	V	V	V
1	2	3	4

The basic ⁴⁄₄ rhythm pattern learnt in **lesson 1** consisted of four down strums (above). After playing the first strum, your right hand moves upwards in preparation for the second strum. The strings are not played on this upward movement. This upward motion can be

represented by a broken upward strum symbol Ʌ which indicates that the strings are not strummed (a silent strum).

So the basic rhythm could be written as:

RHYTHM PATTERN

V	Ʌ	V	Ʌ	V	Ʌ	V	Ʌ
1	+	2	+	3	+	4	+

The above two rhythm patterns sound exactly the same. If you watch your **right** hand you will notice that it actually moves **up and down** in a **continuous motion** but it only makes contact with the strings on the **down** strum. Also, if you play some eighth note rhythms, (see **Lesson 8**) you will see that your right hand also moves up and down in a continuous motion, sometimes making contact with the string and sometimes not.

Silent Strum Symbols

When an **upward** strum is made **without** contacting the strings it can be represented by:

When a **downward** strum is made **without** contacting the strings it can be represented by:

Some very useful and interesting rhythm patterns can result by incorporating eighth note rhythms with silent down strums.

Exercise 49

Try the following rhythm holding a **G** chord. This rhythm is the same as the last eighth note pattern in **lesson 8**, except the down strum on the third beat does not make contact with the strings. You can apply this rhythm to any chord progression you like. This is a very important rhythm and will be the basis of many other rhythms.

RHYTHM PATTERN

V	V	Ʌ	V	Ʌ	V
1	2	+	3	+	4

Try the following variations and make up your own. All these suggested variations are in $\frac{4}{4}$ time but the same principle can be applied to $\frac{3}{4}$ time. Also note that in all these rhythms your **right** hand moves up and down in a **continuous** motion. These rhythm patterns sound "off the beat". This is called **syncopation**.

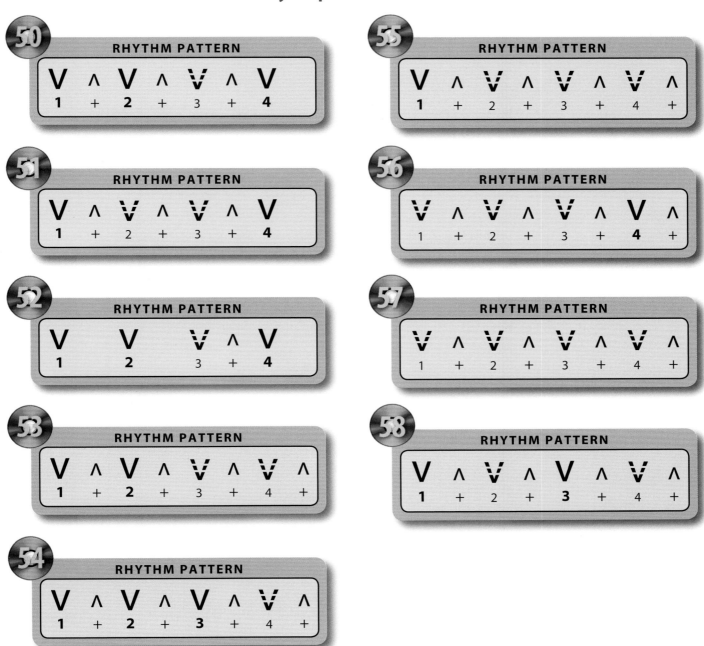

Once you can play these rhythms with a single chord, try applying them to some chord progressions from earlier in the book, e.g. a Turnaround progression. When learning the chords to a new song, try a variety of rhythms with the progression and choose one which sounds good to you.

Exercise 59

Sloop John B

The following song **Sloop John B** is a well known American folk song. Bar 13 uses a tie within the bar connecting an eighth note with a quarter note. This gives the melody a "syncopated" feel. This song is in $\frac{4}{4}$ time and is in the key of **G major**.

Identifying Eighth Note Rhythms

There is a simple system for identifying any note's position in a bar. The system works as follows: within a bar of continuous eighth notes in $\frac{4}{4}$ time, there are eight possible places where notes could occur.

The **first** beat is called **one** (**1**), the next eighth note is called the **"and of 1"**, then comes beat **two** (**2**), the next eighth note is called the **"and of 2"**, then beat **three**, followed by the **"and of 3"**, then beat four, followed by the **"and of 4"** which is the final eighth note in the bar.

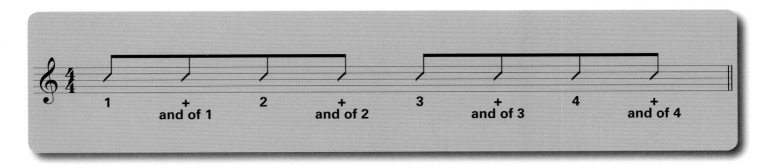

This system is particularly useful if you are having trouble with the timing of a rhythm (e.g. **syncopated rhythms**). You simply identify where the notes occur in relation to each beat and then count them slowly until you have memorized the rhythm.

Later in the book, you will learn rhythms based on smaller subdivisions of the beat such as sixteenth notes. If you have a good understanding of these eighth note positions, the same system can be applied to more complex rhythms, making them easier to learn.

Guitar Effects...

THE WAH WAH PEDAL

The Wah Wah pedal imitates the "Wah" sound used by Jazz trumpeters waving a mute in front of the trumpet. It is a great expression tool for the electric guitar, enabling the guitarist to create talking and crying sounds by moving the foot up and down on the pedal. The Wah Wah pedal was made famous by Jimi Hendrix. He used a model called the "Cry Baby" which is shown in the accompanying photo.

Lesson 23

A flat sign written before a note on the staff means that you play the note that is one fret lower than the note written. For example, the note written on the staff below is called **B flat** (B♭), and is played on the **third** fret of the **3rd** string. When a flat sign is written on the staff, it is always written **before** a note.

Flat Signs

This is a **flat** sign.

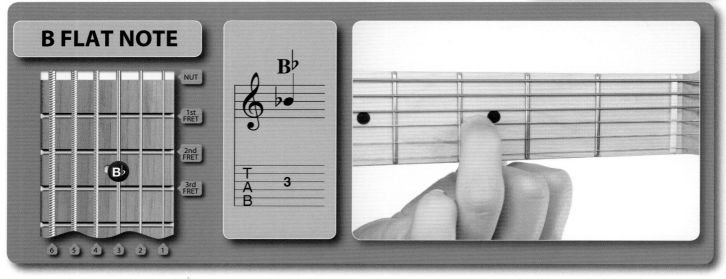

To play the note **B flat** (B♭) place the **third finger** of your left hand just behind the **third fret** of the **3rd string**.

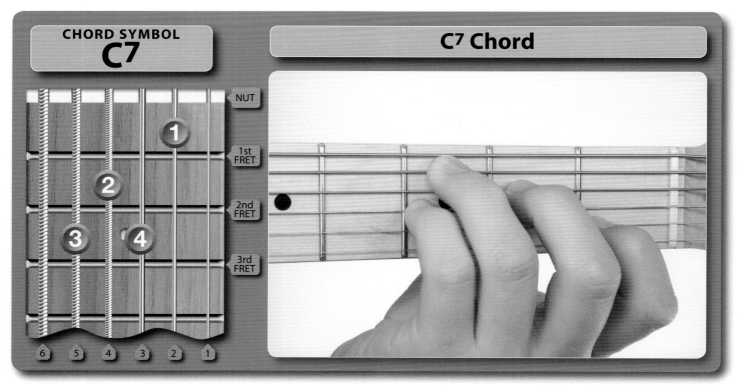

To play the **C7** chord, use the **fourth** fingers of your **left** hand as shown in the diagram, and strum all **six** strings. The C7 chord is a **C** chord with a **B♭** note added.

12 Bar Blues in G

The following Blues progression contains a B♭ note and a C7 chord. The numbers written next to the music notes are **left hand fingering numbers** which indicate the most practical fingering for the example.

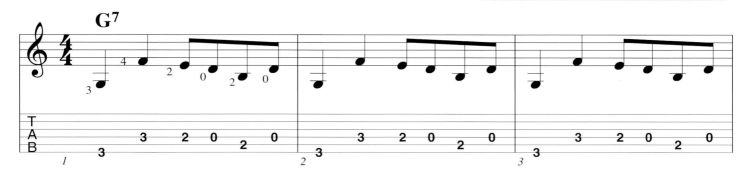

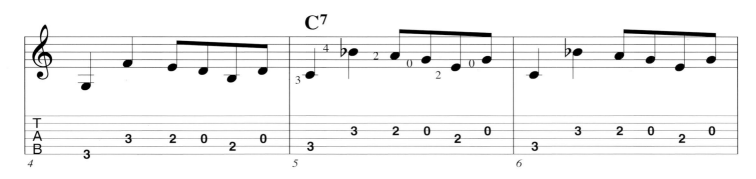

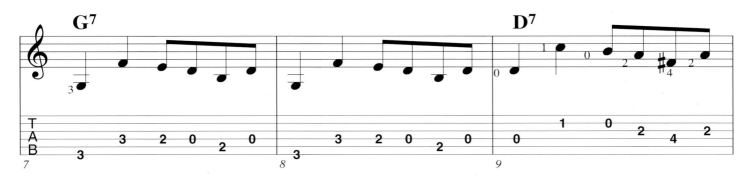

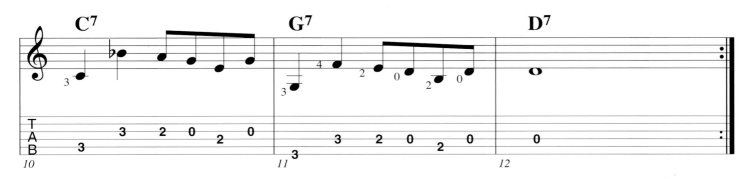

Lesson 24

Key of A Minor

Another easy key for guitarists to play in is **A minor**. The most common chords in the key of **A minor** are **Am, C, Dm, Em, F, G** and **E7**.

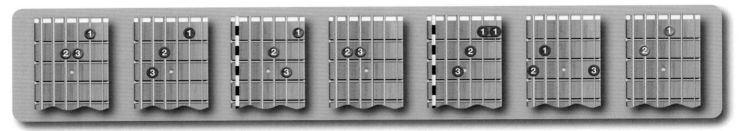

The key signature for the key of **A minor** is the same as **C major** i.e. it contains no sharps or flats.

 **Exercise 61**

Scarborough Fair

This English folk song is in the key of **A minor**. The melody contains an F♯ note in bar 8. Use your fourth finger to play this note. The abbreviation **rit.** above bar 18 indicates to gradually slow down.

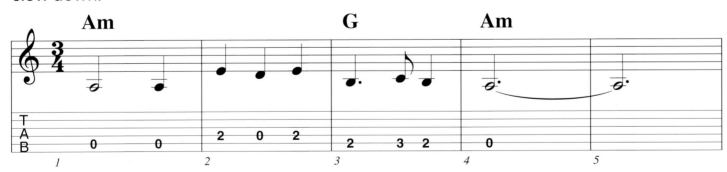

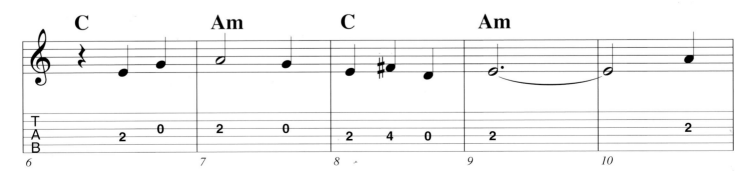

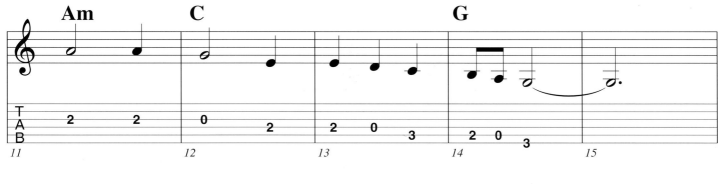

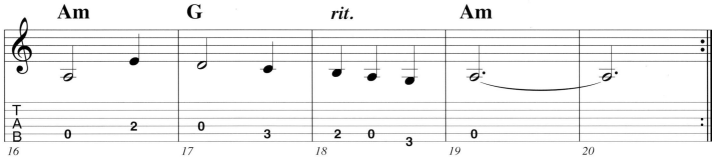

Fingerpicking Guitar

Folk songs like **Scarborough Fair** sound great when accompanied by chords that are fingerpicked on acoustic guitar. Fingerpicking is used in many styles of music including Folk, Blues, Ragtime, Country, Jazz, and World Music.
To learn more about Fingerpicking, visit **www.learntoplaymusic.com**

Know your Guitars…
Martin Dreadnought

In the early part of the 20th century, guitar manufacturer C.F. Martin released an acoustic guitar with a larger, deeper body than most existing guitars. Around the same time, the British navy launched a battleship that was so big it would fear nothing. It was called "HMS Dreadnought". Martin thought this would be a good name for his new guitar. The guitar sounded great and the name caught on. Today, the dreadnought is the most commonly used type of acoustic guitar in the world.

Exercise 62

Greensleeves

Greensleeves is an old English folk song which has been used in the sound tracks of many motion pictures and television shows. It is in the key of **A minor**.

The melody contains **F♯** and **G♯** notes. The G♯ note is a part of the **E7** chord shape and is on the first fret of the 3rd string.

Songs in the key of **A minor** often contain F♯ and/or G♯ notes. The suggested rhythm uses a bass note rhythm pattern in ¾ time. The bass note to play is the root note of the chord. e.g. for an **A minor** chord pick the open 5th string (an A note).

The sharp sign (or flat sign) affects **all** notes of that name within the bar in which it appears. e.g. in bars **10** and **26** of Greensleeves the ♯ sign appears before the first **G** note in each bar. The sharp also applies to all other G notes within that particular bar.

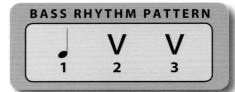

The effect of a sharp or flat sign is **cancelled by a bar line**, meaning that a **new** sign would be needed to indicate any sharps or flats in the following bar.

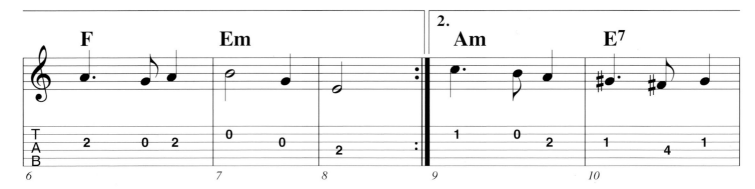

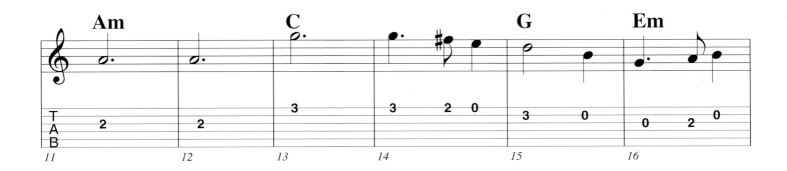

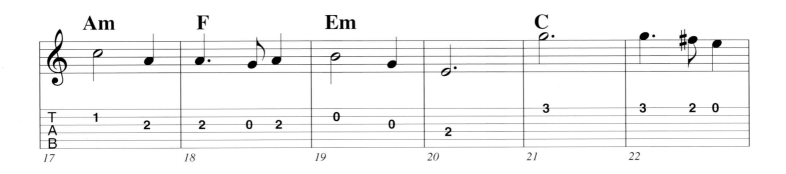

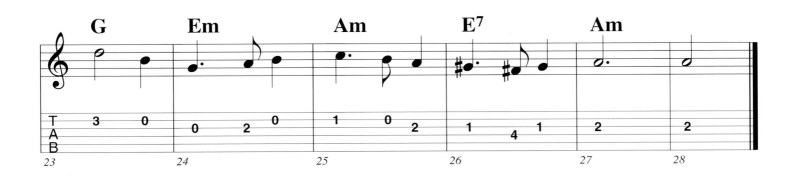

Amplifiers...
THE FENDER TWIN
The most famous of all combo amps is the Fender Twin Reverb. It produces a crisp clean tone, even at high volumes and is used by players of many different musical styles. Many players use a Fender Twin as their basic sound and combine it with pedals to achieve distortion and other effects.

Lesson 25

The Eighth Rest

This symbol is a **eighth rest**. It indicates **half a beat** of silence.

If a rest comes after you have played a note, you must stop the note sounding.

To do this, lift your finger off the fret but keep it lightly touching the string.

To stop an open string sounding, lightly touch it with any finger of your left hand.

Exercise 63

El Condor Pasa

This song from South America is also in the key of **A minor**. Eighth rests are used throughout. The melody contains **G♯** notes and uses a new **A note** on the fifth fret of the 1st string. Play this high A note with the **fourth** finger of your left hand.

RHYTHM PATTERN

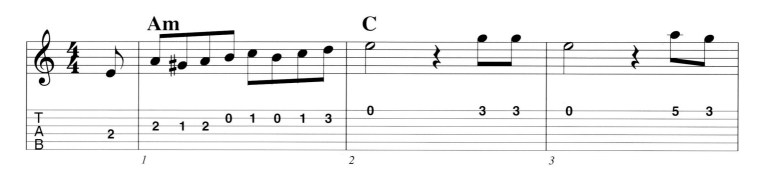

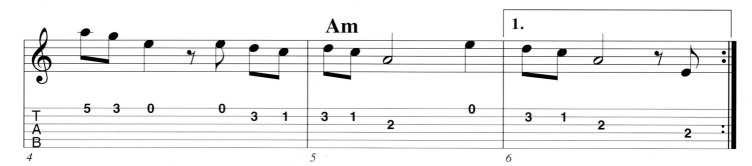

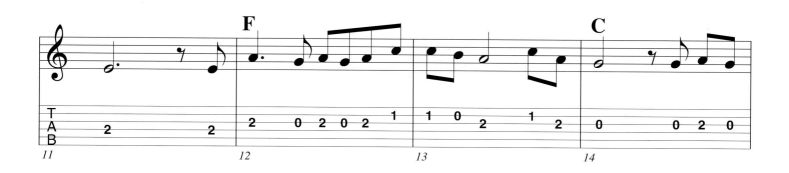

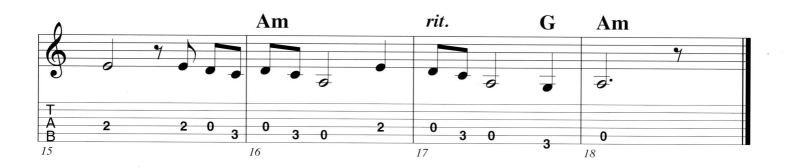

Know your Guitars...

RICKENBACKER 12 STRING

The electric guitar was invented by Adolf Rickenbacker in the 1930's. Rickenbacker guitars are now commonly used in Rock and Pop music. The Rickenbacker 12 string was made famous by George Harrison of the Beatles. It is also used by Roger McGuinn of the Byrds and by Tom Petty. 12 string guitars contain six courses of two strings side by side, with the two strings tuned an octave apart. The 12 string has a singing quality and is great for both chords and picking melodies.

Lesson 26

The Six Eight Time Signature

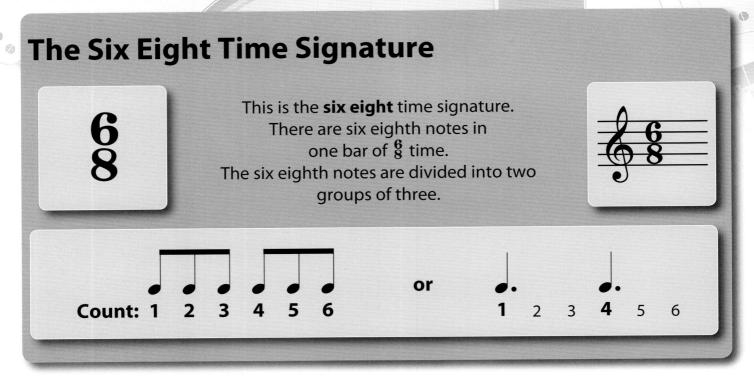

6/8

This is the **six eight** time signature. There are six eighth notes in one bar of **6/8** time. The six eighth notes are divided into two groups of three.

Count: 1 2 3 4 5 6 **or** 1 2 3 4 5 6

When playing **6/8** time there are **two** beats within each bar, with each beat being a **dotted quarter note**. (This is different to **4/4** and **3/4** time where each beat is a quarter note). **Accent** (play louder) the 1 and 4 count to help establish the two beats per bar.

 Exercise 64

House of the Rising Sun

This song is in **6/8** time and is in the **key of A minor**. It contains a G♯ note in bar 14 and the high A note introduced in t last song. The suggested rhythm pattern is in **6/8** time. Accent the strums on the 1 and 4 counts to help keep time.

SUGGESTED RHYTHM PATTERN

V	V	∧	V	∧	V	V	V
1	2	+	3	+	4	5	6

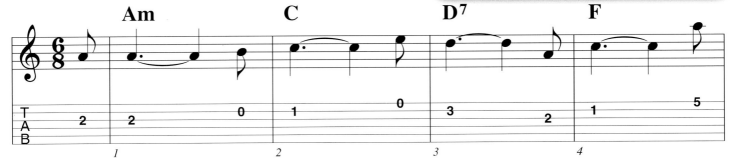

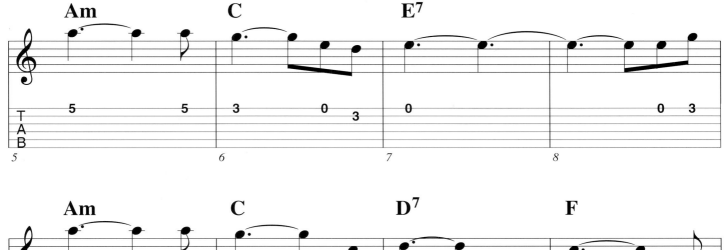

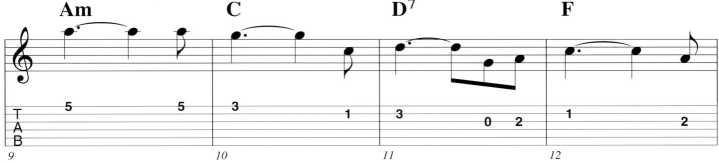

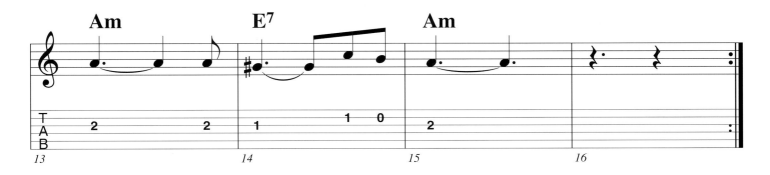

Simple and Compound Time

Time signatures fall into two basic categories – simple time and compound time. Simple time is any time signature where the basic beat is divisible by two. E.g. in $\frac{2}{4}$, $\frac{4}{4}$, and $\frac{2}{2}$ the basic beat is a quarter note, which may be divided in half to become two eighth notes per beat.

Any time signature where the basic beat is divisible by three is called compound time. The most common example of compound time is six eight time ($\frac{6}{8}$). Other examples of compound are $\frac{9}{8}$ and $\frac{12}{8}$. In compound time, the basic beat is felt as a dotted quarter note which can be divided by three.

When Johnny Comes Marching Home

This song dates back to the American civil war. It is in $\frac{6}{8}$ time and in the key of **A minor**.
The suggested rhythm for this song is a half note strum pattern which lasts for the whole six beats of the bar. In bars 13 and 14 you will need to strum twice per bar because there are two chords in these bars. This requires the use of two **dotted quarter note strums**.
Since a dot placed after a note or strum extends its value by half, the dotted quarter note strum lasts for the same time as three eighth notes.
This means that two dotted quarter note strums fit exactly with the two dotted quarter note beats in one bar of $\frac{6}{8}$ time.

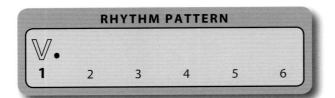

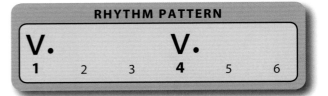

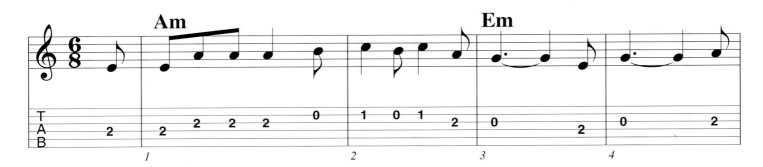

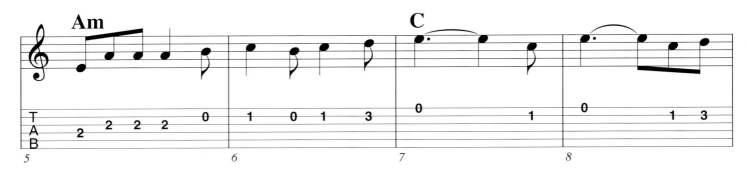

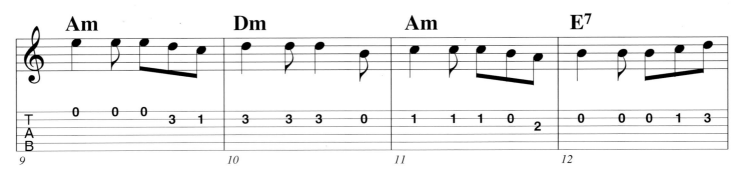

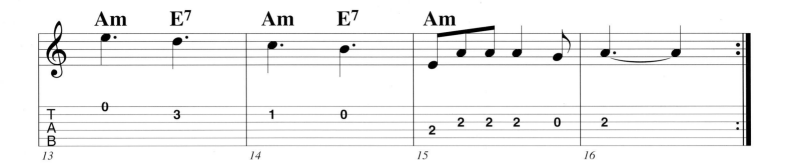

Tempo Markings

The term **tempo** refers to the **speed** at which music is played. Tempo markings come from Italian words. Some of these are listed below, along with their English translations. It is important to be able to recognize these markings and to be able to comfortably play music at each tempo.

adagio (slowly)   *andante* (an easy walking pace)   *moderato* (a moderate speed)

allegro (fast)   *presto* (very fast)

Tempo Changes

There are also specific markings for changes in tempo. The most common of these are listed below.

rallentando
accelerando (gradually becoming faster)   or   (gradually becoming slower)
ritardando

ritenuto (**rit**) (immediately slower)   *a tempo* (return to the original tempo)
- This one appears in the song
El Condor Pasa on page 92.

There are many other traditional musical terms which it is useful to know, especially when playing with Classical or Jazz musicians. To learn more about musical terms, see the **dictionary of musical terms** at the end of this book, or visit **www.learntoplaymusic.com**

Lesson 27

Notes on the Guitar Fretboard

Across the bottom of the page spread is a fretboard diagram of all the notes on the guitar. Play the notes on each string from the open notes to the 12th fret. The note on the 12th fret is one octave higher than the open note e.g. the open 6th string is an **E** note and the note on the 12th fret of the 6th string is also an **E** note, but is one octave higher.

Sharps and Flats

A **sharp** (♯) raises the pitch of a note by one semitone (1 fret). A **flat** (♭) lowers the pitch of a note by one semitone. In music notation the ♯ and ♭ signs are placed before the note on the staff.

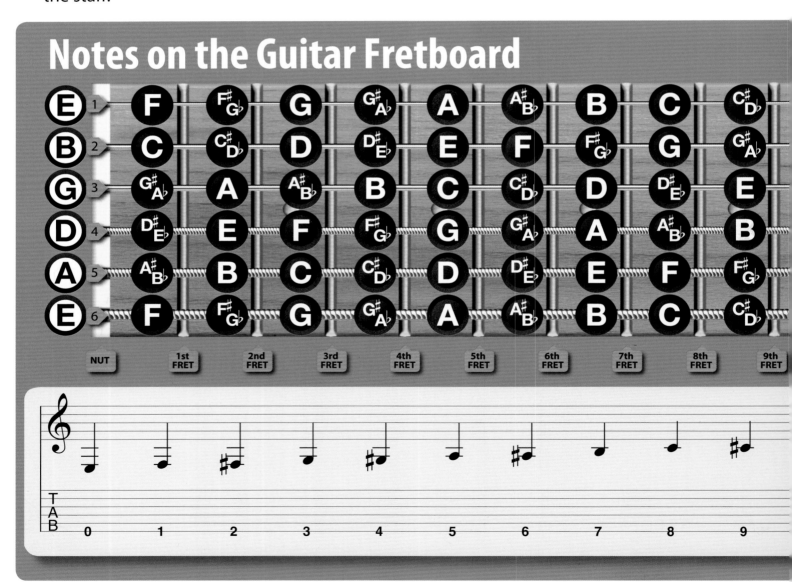

www.learntoplaymusic.com

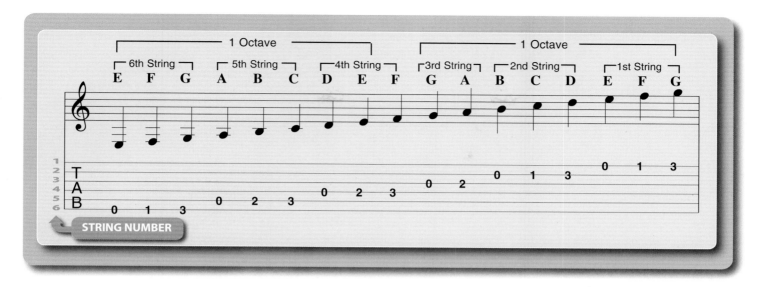

The **open position** of the guitar contains the notes of the open strings in the first three frets. Outlined above are the position of these notes on the staff, tab, and on the fretboard. Also shown is an example of two separate **octaves**, an octave being two notes that have the same letter name and are eight consecutive notes apart. All the songs and examples in this book use notes in the open position.

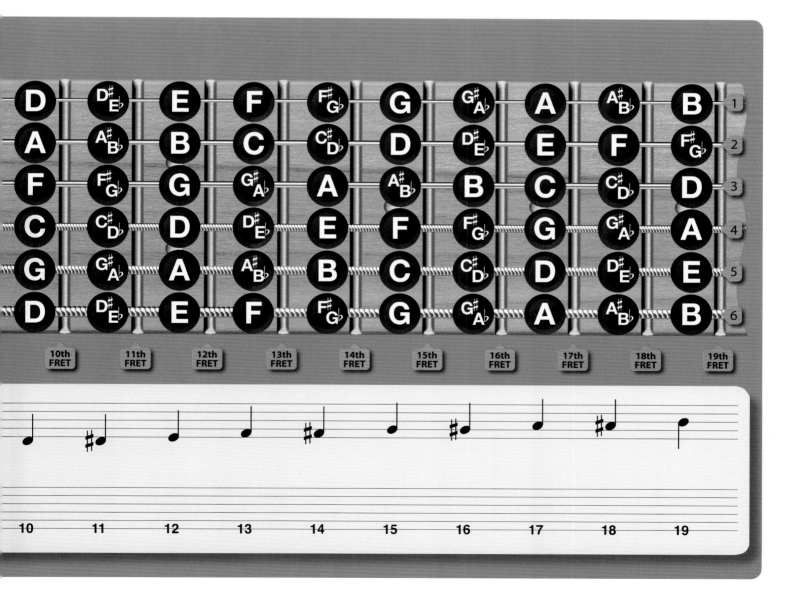

The Chromatic Scale

With the inclusion of sharps and flats, there are 12 different notes within one octave, as shown below. The notes (**E and F**) and (**B and C**) are always one semitone apart (1 fret). The other notes are a tone apart (2 frets). Sharps (#) and flats (♭) are found between the notes that are a tone apart:

| C | C#/D♭ | D | D#/E♭ | EF | F#/G♭ | G | G#/A♭ | A | A#/B♭ | BC |

This scale is called the **chromatic scale** and contains all the sharps (#'s) and flats (♭'s) possible. **C sharp** (C#) has the same position on the fretboard as **D flat** (D♭).
They are the same note but can have different names depending upon what key you are playing in. The same applies to D#/E♭, F#/G♭, G#/A♭ and A#/B♭. These are called **enharmonic notes**. Written on the previous pages are all the notes on the **guitar** including these sharps and flats.

Also notice that: The **5th fret of the 6th string** (A note) is the same note as the **open 5th string**.
The **5th fret of the 5th string** (D note) is the same note as the **open 4th string**.
The **5th fret of the 4th string** (G note) is the same note as the **open 3rd string**.
The **4th fret of the 3rd string** (B note) is the same note as the **open 2nd string**.
The **5th fret of the 2nd string** (E note) is the same note as the **open 1st string**.

These note positions are important to remember because they are the basis for tuning your guitar to itself (see page 106).

Exercise 66

Hall of the Mountain King

Hall of the Mountain King contains many chromatic notes. Remember that the sharp sign (or flat sign) affects **ALL** notes of that name within the bar in which it appears.

E.g. in bars 3 and 19 the first note of the bar is B♭. The flat sign written next to this note also affects the third note in the bar. Similarly, in bars 10, 12, 14 and 25 there is a sharp written before the first note of the bar. This sharp affects all other notes of the same name within these bars.

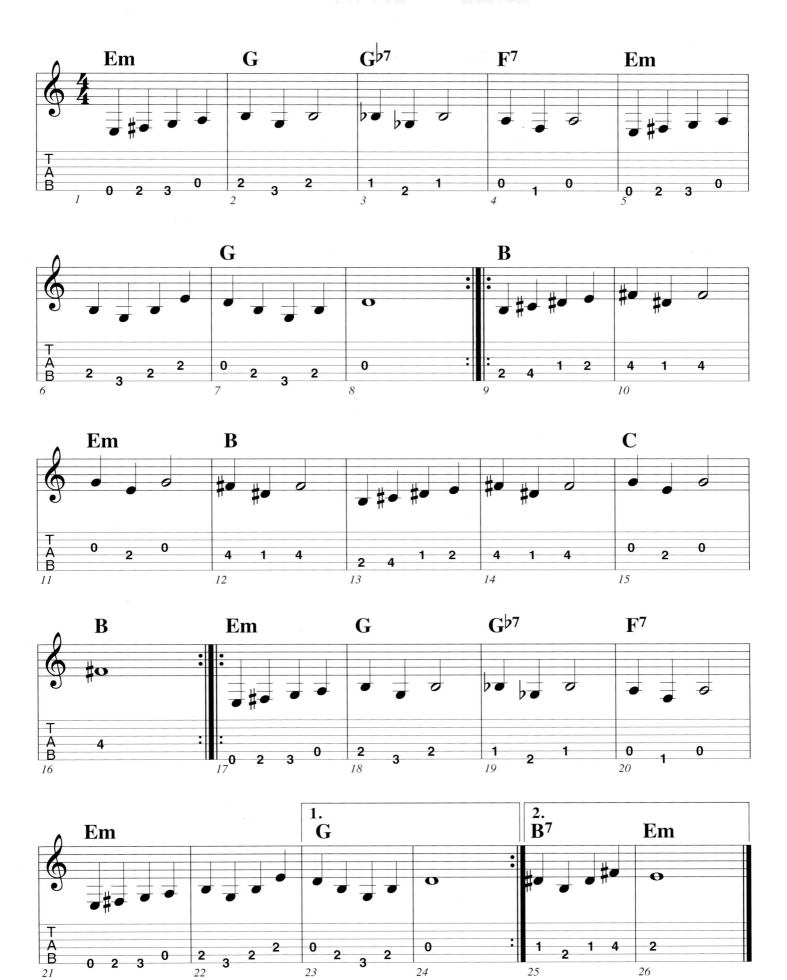

Tuning Methods

There are many different ways to tune the guitar, with some methods being more accurate than others. Some methods are relatively simple to use and some methods can be quite difficult, requiring a great deal of practice. The most popular methods of tuning the guitar will be covered in detail throughout the following pages.

Using an Electronic Tuner

Electronic Tuner

The easiest and most accurate way to tune your guitar is by using an **electronic tuner**. An electronic tuner allows you to tune each string individually to the tuner, by indicating whether the notes are sharp (too high) or flat (too low). There are basically two types of electronic tuners. One type uses the position of a needle to indicate the correct pitch of a note and the other type uses a row of lights to indicate the correct pitch of a note. Most electronic tuners are relatively inexpensive and simple to operate.

TUNING ACOUSTIC GUITARS
Most tuners will have an inbuilt microphone so if you have another Acoustic Guitar, all you will need to do is place the tuner close to the body of the guitar and pick each string.
Pick each string cleanly. Do not pick the string aggressively, as an incorrect reading will be given. Sometimes the needle of the tuner's meter or the lights will move unevenly and make the tuner difficult to use. This can be caused by several things;

1. The inbuilt microphone is not picking up the sound of the string enough. Experiment with the distance between the tuner and the body of the guitar.
2. The tuner could be picking up other sounds in the room. Ensure the room is quiet.
3. Make sure the battery is fully powered. It is easy to forget to turn off a tuner and as a battery gets flat a poor reading will be given.
4. Check that you are tuning the correct note, sometimes a string can be so out of tune that the tuner will mistake it for the wrong string.

TUNING ELECTRIC GUITARS

If you have an electric guitar you can plug it directly into the tuner. The tuner has a normal guitar input jack that enables you to connect your guitar lead. Most guitar tuners also have an extra hole allowing you to connect your tuner inline between your guitar and amplifier. Ensure that your guitar is plugged into the input jack and not the output jack that goes to the amplifier. Other things to consider when using an electronic tuner are:

1. The volume control should be turned up, otherwise the tuner will not receive any signal and not register. Experiment between the volume of your guitar and how strongly you pick the string. Some tuners prefer not to receive a signal that is too strong.

2. Set your pick-up switch. Use your pick-up that is closest to your neck and not the bridge.

3. As you pick a string, try to stop the other strings sounding by touching them lightly with your left hand. This will stop the tuner hearing any 'overtones' from the other strings.

Tuning Your Guitar to Another Guitar

If you have another guitar that is in tune you will be able to tune your guitar to it. Position yourself close to the other guitar in a quiet location.

1. Have someone pick the sixth string of the other guitar.

2. Listen carefully to the string, and try to focus on to the sound and pitch of the note.

3. While still focusing on that note, play the sixth string of your guitar and try to determine whether the sixth string on your guitar is higher in pitch or lower in pitch than the other string.

4. If you think the note is too low you will need to tighten your sixth string by turning its tuning key in an anti-clockwise direction. If you think the note is too high you will need to loosen your sixth string by turning its tuning key in a clockwise direction.

5. Double check that you are about to turn the correct tuning key. Play the sixth string again and turn the tuning key. Listen for the sound of the string rising or lowering in pitch.

6. When you are satisfied that the notes are both the same, continue with the other strings until all six strings have been tuned.

TUNING TIPS:

• You may find it easier to start with the first string rather than the sixth string.

• It is a good idea to always tune up to a note rather than down to a note. If you think the note is too high and needs to be lowered, detune the string so it is lower than the desired pitch, then tune up to the desired pitch. In most cases you will find this easier and more accurate. Tuning up to the note also puts pressure on the tuning key, keeping the string in tune longer.

• The above method is perfect for practising tuning if the other person is a competent tuner. They will be able to supervise you and check your tuning afterwards.

Tuning Your Guitar to the CD or DVD

The DVD contains a tuning menu, and the first 6 tracks on the accompanying CDs contain recordings of the open strings of a guitar. On each track a string is played several times, giving you sufficient time to tune the corresponding string on your guitar to the sound of the note on the recording. You may also be able to program your player to repeat a specific track several times, increasing the amount of times the note can be heard. The recording contains open string tuning notes for steel string acoustic and electric guitars. Beginners may find it easier to tune the strings of their guitar to the corresponding type of guitar on the recording. Each type of guitar has its own particular tonal characteristics and first time tuners will be able to hear the sound of a string that best matches the sound of their instrument. As with all tuning methods, make sure you practice tuning to the recording in a quiet environment and double check that you are adjusting the correct tuning key before turning.

Checking Your Tuning With a Chord

Once you are confident you have tuned all your strings, it is a good idea to check your tuning by strumming a chord. Hold an open E Major chord as shown below and slowly strum across the strings.

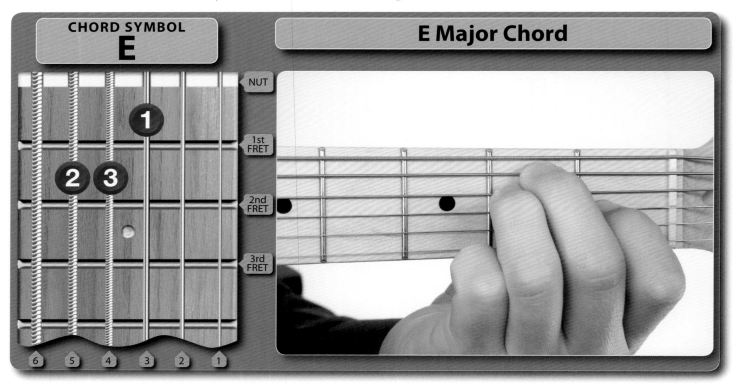

CHORD SYMBOL
E

E Major Chord

Tuning Your Guitar to a Piano or Keyboard

Sometimes you may need to play along with another instrument. In these cases it is essential that your guitar be in tune with that instrument. Tune the open strings of your guitar to the corresponding notes of the accompanying instrument. For example to tune to a piano, tune the open 6th string to the E note on the piano, as shown on the keyboard diagram. Then either tune your guitar to itself from this note using the methods outlined on the following pages, or tune each string of your guitar to those notes of the piano shown on the diagram.

To check if your guitar is in tune, strum a **G chord** (see **Lesson 1**). Most students find it easier to tune up to a note, so you may wish to detune your string to a pitch slightly below the recording, and tune up from there.

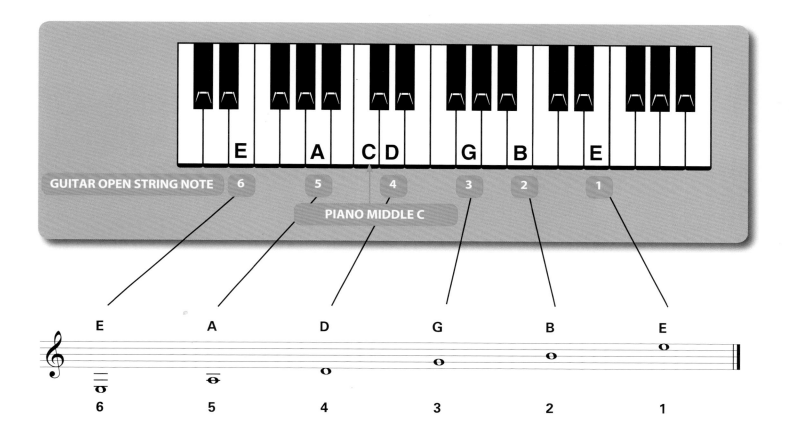

Tuning the Guitar to Itself

The methods outlined on the previous pages involved comparing each individual string to another note. However it is essential that you are able to tune the guitar to itself, meaning it is important to be able to check each string with the other strings on the guitar.

The following method requires the sixth string to be already in tune. If it is not possible to have the sixth string in tune using one of the methods discussed, it may be necessary to seek assistance with getting the sixth string as close as possible to concert pitch. It is acceptable to tune the guitar to itself, though it may not be at concert pitch, i.e. in tune with other instruments.

The most important thing to consider with this method is that the pitch of your sixth string must not be too far below or too far above concert pitch. Remember that if your guitar has already been correctly tuned and you have followed correct maintenance procedure as outlined earlier, your strings should only require minor tuning. Therefore your guitar should not be too far below or above concert pitch.

Once you are satisfied with the pitch of the sixth string, the following steps should be followed:

STEP 1   TUNING THE 5TH STRING TO THE 6TH STRING

Place a left hand finger on the 6th string at the fifth fret, and play the string. Play the open 5th string (an A note). If this note sounds the same as the note you played on the 6th string at the fifth fret, the open 5th string is in tune. If the open 5th string sounds higher, it means that it is sharp. Turn the tuning key slowly in a clockwise direction, therefore lowering the pitch of the note. If the open 5th string sounds lower, it means that it is flat. Turn the tuning key slowly in a counter-clockwise direction, thus raising the pitch of the note.

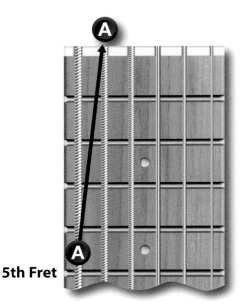

5th Fret

Note: Ensure that you are turning the correct tuning key and listen to the string change pitch as you turn the tuning key. Play the two strings again and compare the notes. Keep doing this until the open A string sounds the same as the A note at the fifth fret of the 6th string.

STEP 2   TUNING THE 4TH STRING TO THE 5TH STRING

Place a left hand finger on the 5th string at the fifth fret, and play the string. Play the open 4th string (a D note). If this note sounds the same as the note you played on the 5th string at the fifth fret, the open 4th string is in tune. If the open 4th string sounds higher, it means that it is sharp. Turn the tuning key slowly in a clockwise direction, therefore lowering the pitch of the note. If the open 4th string sounds lower, it means that it is flat. Turn the tuning key slowly in a counter-clockwise direction, thus raising the pitch of the note. Play the two strings again and compare the notes. Keep doing this until the open D string sounds the same as the D note at the fifth fret of the 5th string.

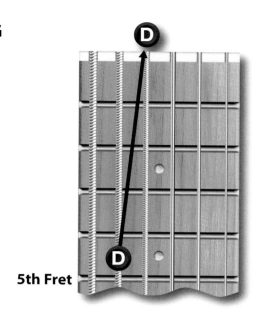

5th Fret

STEP 3   TUNING THE 3RD STRING TO THE 4TH STRING

Now place a left hand finger on the 4th string at the fifth fret, and play the string. Play the open 3rd string (a G note). If this note sounds the same as the note you played on the 4th string at the fifth fret, the open 3rd string is in tune. If the open 3rd string sounds higher, turn the tuning key slowly in a clockwise direction to lower the pitch of the note. If the open 3rd string sounds lower, turn the tuning key slowly in a counter-clockwise direction to raise the pitch of the note. Play the two strings again and compare the notes. Keep doing this until the open G string sounds the same as the G note at the fifth fret of the 4th string.

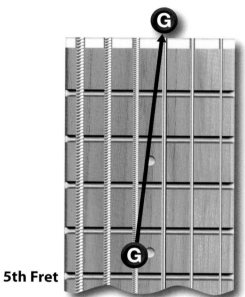

5th Fret

STEP 4   TUNING THE 2ND STRING TO THE 3RD STRING

Now place a left hand finger on the 3rd string at the fourth fret, and play the string. Play the open 2nd string (a B note). If this note sounds the same as the note you played on the 3rd string at the fourth fret, the open 2nd string is in tune. If the open 2nd string sounds higher, turn the tuning key slowly in a clockwise direction to lower the pitch of the note. If the open 2nd string sounds lower, turn the tuning key slowly in a counter-clockwise direction to raise the pitch of the note. Play the two strings again and compare the notes. Keep doing this until the open B string sounds the same as the B note at the fourth fret of the 3rd string.

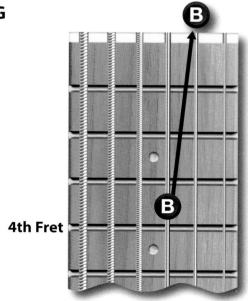

4th Fret

STEP 5   TUNING THE 1ST STRING TO THE 2ND STRING

Finally, place a left hand finger on the 2nd string at the fifth fret, and play the string. Play the open 1st string (an E note). If this note sounds the same as the note you played on the 2nd string at the fifth fret, the open 1st string is in tune. If the open 1st string sounds higher, turn the tuning key slowly in a clockwise direction to lower the pitch of the note. If the open 1st string sounds lower, turn the tuning key slowly in a counter-clockwise direction to raise the pitch of the note. Play the two strings again and compare the notes. Keep doing this until the open E string sounds the same as the E note at the fifth fret of the 2nd string.

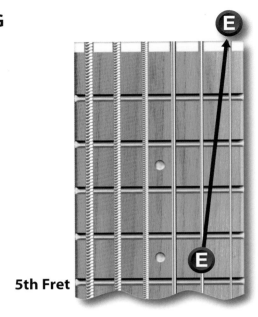

5th Fret

Tuning the Guitar to a Tuning Fork

Tuning your guitar to a tuning fork is one of the least expensive methods of ensuring your guitar will be at concert pitch. A tuning fork is a small metal object in the shape of a fork that is hit against something solid and placed on the bridge or soundboard of the guitar, producing a note that the first string can be tuned to. The other strings are then tuned to the 1st string. The most common tuning fork is an A tuning fork that gives the note A on the 5th fret of the first string. An E tuning fork is also available which produces the note of the open 1st string (E).

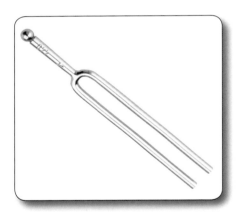

Tuning Fork

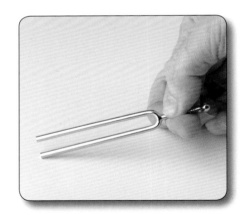

Strike Tuning Fork

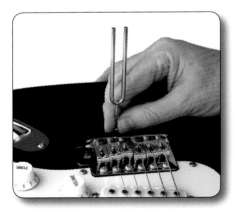

Place Tuning Fork on Guitar

STEP 1   TUNING THE 1ST STRING TO THE TUNING FORK

Play either the open 1st string (E), or the fifth fret of the 1st string (A) depending on which tuning fork you have. Immediately after picking the string, strike the tuning fork against something solid and place the fork on the bridge of the guitar. Compare the pitch of the string and the sound produced by the tuning fork. If the pitch of the tuning fork sounds the same as the note you played on the 1st string, the string is in tune. If the 1st string sounds higher, it means that it is sharp. Turn the tuning key slowly in a clockwise direction, therefore lowering the pitch of the note. If the 1st string sounds lower, it means that it is flat. Turn the tuning key slowly in a counter-clockwise direction to raise the pitch of the note.

STEP 2   TUNING THE 2ND STRING TO THE 1ST STRING

The next step is to tune the rest of the strings to the 1st string. This is done in the same way as tuning the guitar to itself, as explained on the previous pages, except the strings are tuned in the reverse order. Place a left hand finger on the 2nd string at the fifth fret, and play the string. Play the open 1st string. This time you will need to tune the 2nd string to the pitch of the 1st string. Turn the tuning key for the 2nd string in the correct direction, as explained in step 1, until the note on the fifth fret of the 2nd string (E) is the same as the open 1st string (E).

STEP 3   TUNING THE 3RD STRING TO THE 2ND STRING

Place a left hand finger on the 3rd string at the 4th fret, and play the string. Play the open 2nd string. Adjust the tuning key for the 3rd string until the note on the fourth fret of the 3rd string (B) is the same as the open 2nd string (B).

STEP 4   TUNING THE 4TH STRING TO THE 3RD STRING

Place a left hand finger on the 4th string at the 5th fret, and play the string. Play the open 3rd string. Adjust the tuning key for the 4th string until the note on the fifth fret of the 4th string (G) is the same as the open 3rd string (G).

STEP 5   TUNING THE 5TH STRING TO THE 4TH STRING

Place a left hand finger on the 5th string at the 5th fret, and play the string. Play the open 4th string. Adjust the tuning key for the 5th string until the note on the fifth fret of the 5th string (D) is the same as the open 4th string (D).

STEP 6   TUNING THE 6TH STRING TO THE 5TH STRING

Finally place a left hand finger on the 6th string at the 5th fret, and play the string. Play the open 5th string. Adjust the tuning key for the 6th string until the note on the fifth fret of the 6th string (A) is the same as the open 5th string (A). This step and each of the previous steps can be shown in the adjacent diagram.

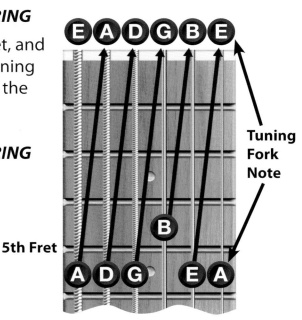

Before You Begin to Tune Your Guitar

The following tips will greatly improve your chances of successfully tuning your guitar.

Tuning New Strings

If you are a beginner and have fitted new strings to your guitar, it is recommended you get some assistance at first from an experienced guitar player. It is at this stage of tuning that the risk of breaking a string is highest. Once the strings are fitted and tuned you will find it easier to keep the guitar in tune by using minor adjustments.

'Working In' New Strings

New strings will need to be 'worked in' after each fitting. This is especially helpful if you are fitting one new string at a time and you would like the string to stay in tune before fitting the next string.

Strings should be stretched by pulling them away from the fretboard a little. The string can also be stretched in sections along the string by stretching the string between the thumb and fingers of your right hand. Obviously do not over stretch the string as you could break the string. Ask an experienced guitarist for a lesson in this technique.

Once a string is fitted it should also be played a little to help with the settling down of the string. Sometimes it can take a few days for a new string to settle in but once it has, it should maintain its tuning and only require minor adjustments.

Room Acoustics and Temperature

The sound of the room will assist with tuning. Try to tune the guitar in a quiet room so you can clearly hear the pitch and tone of each note as you are tuning. A useful tip is to practice tuning in the bathroom which often has the best acoustics in the house, helping to produce a strong, clear note.

Try to keep your guitar at a constant temperature. Moving your instrument from a cold room to a warmer room, or visa versa, can effect the pitch of the strings.

Slowly at First!

At the early stages of learning how to tune the guitar it is vital to approach it slowly and very carefully. A common error is to turn the wrong tuning key, causing another string that perhaps has already been tuned to be put out of tune. It also creates the risk of breaking a string. Before you adjust a tuning key, double check that you will in fact be turning the correct tuning key.

If your guitar has already been tuned, perhaps by your teacher or a friend, you should only need to make minor adjustments to the tuning key. Therefore it should not be necessary to turn the tuning key very much at all. If you find yourself turning a tuning key a lot, pause and rethink what you are doing. Chances are you could be doing something incorrectly.

Patience

Everyone has trouble with tuning a guitar in the beginning. Be patient and eventually you will be tuning your guitar, quickly, easily and accurately.

   www.learntoplaymusic.com

Chord Charts

The following pages contain charts of the types of chords you will most commonly find in sheet music. Most of the shapes given are based around the first few frets. Many of the shapes were shown earlier in the book and are easy to play. These open chords sound particularly good on acoustic guitars and for fingerpicking. The other shapes are given for your reference but in most cases would be better played holding a bar chord shape. Bar chords, although a little difficult at first are ultimately easier and more convenient to play than most of the non-outlined shapes. All good guitarists play bar chords. These final chord charts will give you an introduction to moveable Jazz chord shapes. Some of these chords are less common but sound great and will increase your chord vocabulary.

Types of Chord Shapes

Open Chords

Chord shapes can be divided into three common types. The ones you have learnt up to this point are called **open chords** because they contain open strings (i.e. no finger is placed on the fret). Open chords are the most important ones to learn first because they are the most common, and most other types of chords are derived from these open chords. There are many thousands of songs which contain only open chords.

Bar Chords

A **Bar chord** has no open strings and can be played anywhere on the fretboard. The first finger of the left hand is used to Bar across all six strings of one fret, and the other fingers are used to form the chord shape. You will learn how to play bar chords in this section of the book. The root note of each Bar chord is indicated by a white dot. Bar chords are commonly used in **Pop**, **Rock** and **Blues** music, and when played on an electric guitar with loud volume and amplifier distortion Bar chords (and parts of Bar chords called power chords) are the basis of heavier rock styles, e.g. **Heavy Metal**. Bar chords are easier to play on an electric guitar but are also played on acoustic guitars. Bar chord shapes are called **Moveable** shapes because they can be played with the first finger bar on any fret.

Jazz Chords

Other types of moveable chord shapes are **Jazz chord** shapes. As the name suggests they are commonly used in Jazz music. Generally they are harder to play, but songs and chord progressions containing Jazz chord shapes have a unique sound that cannot be achieved with open or Bar chords. You can find some Jazz chord shapes in the chord charts at the end of the book. To learn more about Jazz chords, visit **www.learntoplaymusic.com**

Major Chords

Major chords are constructed from the **1st**, **3rd** and **5th** degrees of the Major scale.

e.g. **C**

Scale Degree	1	2	3	4	5	6	7	8
Note Name	C	D	E	F	G	A	B	C
Chord Formula	1		3		5			
Notes in Chord	C		E		G			

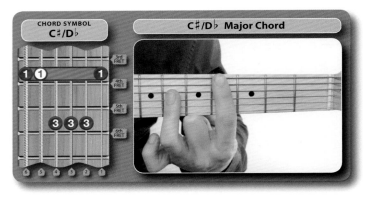

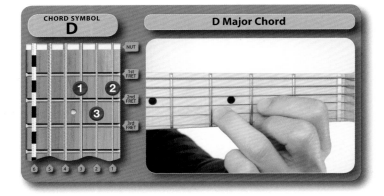

Major Chords

CHORD SYMBOL

maj

MAJOR

CHORD FORMULA

1   3   5

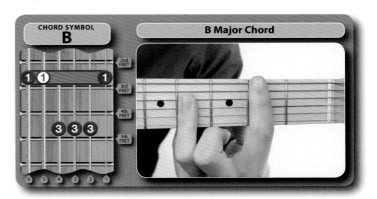

Minor Chords

Minor chords are constructed from the **1st**, **flat 3rd**, and **5th** degrees of the Major scale.

e.g. **Cm**

Scale Degree	1	2	3	4	5	6	7	8
Note Name	C	D	E	F	G	A	B	C
Chord Formula	1		♭3		5			
Notes in Chord	C		E♭		G			

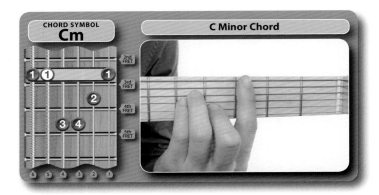

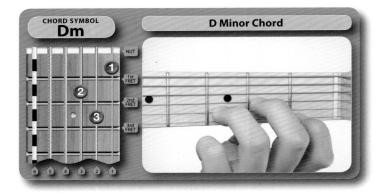

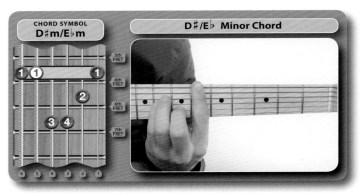

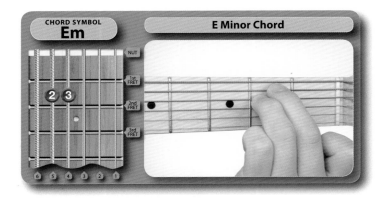

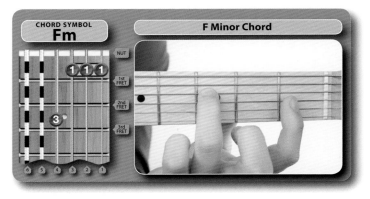

www.learntoplaymusic.com

Minor Chords

MINOR

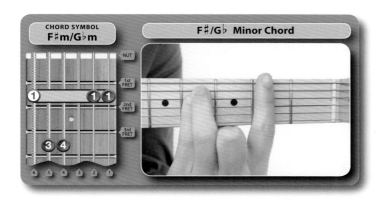

F#/G♭ Minor Chord

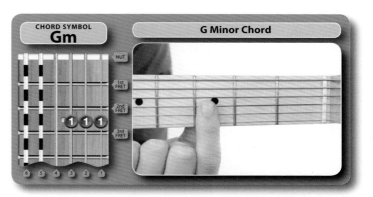

G Minor Chord

G#/A♭ Minor Chord

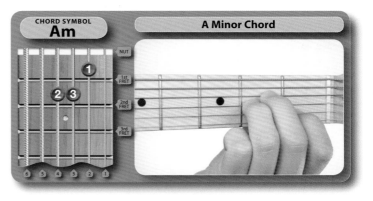

A Minor Chord

A#/B♭ Minor Chord

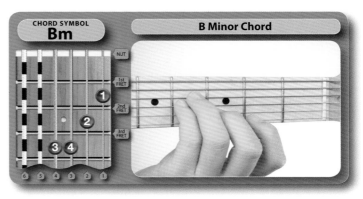

B Minor Chord

Dominant Seventh Chords

Dominant Seventh chords are constructed from the **1st, 3rd, 5th** and **flat 7th** degrees of the Major scale.

e.g. **C⁷**

Scale Degree	1	2	3	4	5	6	7	8
Note Name	C	D	E	F	G	A	B	C
Chord Formula	1		3		5		♭7	
Notes in Chord	C		E		G		B♭	

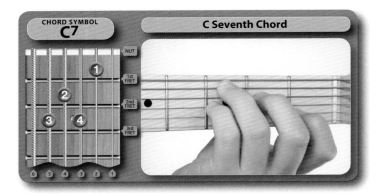

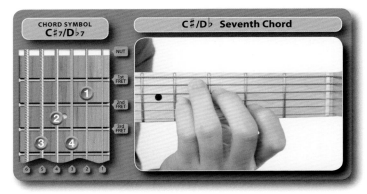

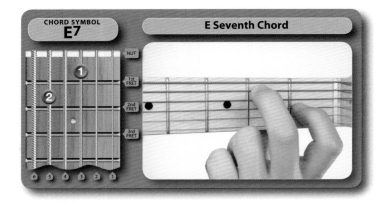

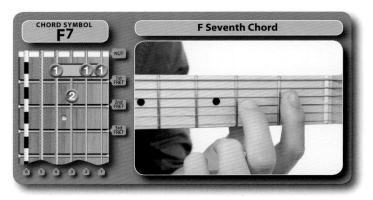

Dominant Seventh Chords

CHORD SYMBOL

7

DOMINANT SEVENTH

CHORD FORMULA

$1 \quad 3 \quad 5 \quad \flat 7$

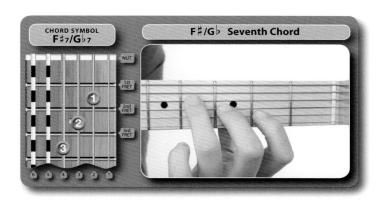

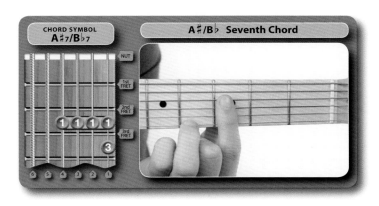

*Some guitarists prefer to deaden the 6th string with their thumb as pictured.

Suspended Chords

Suspended chords are constructed from the **1st, 4th,** and **5th** degrees of the Major scale.

e.g. **Csus**

Scale Degree	1	2	3	4	5	6	7	8
Note Name	C	D	E	F	G	A	B	C
Chord Formula	1			4	5			
Notes in Chord	C			F	G			

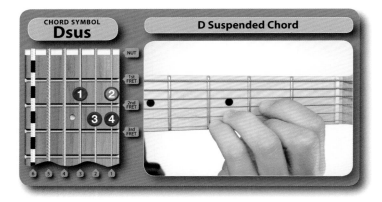

www.learntoplaymusic.com

Suspended Chords

sus

SUSPENDED

CHORD FORMULA

1   4   5

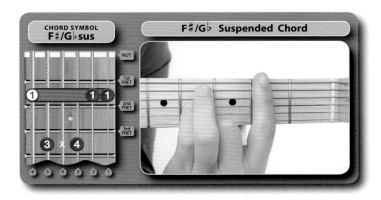

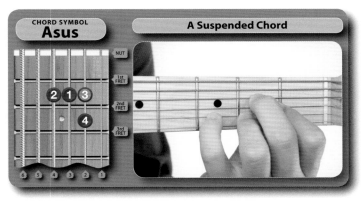

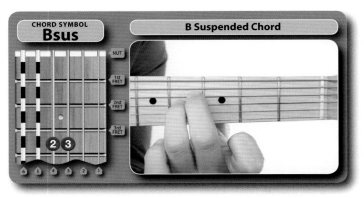

Augmented Chords

Augmented chords are constructed from the **1st**, **3rd**, and **sharp 5th** degrees of the Major scale.

e.g. **Caug**

Scale Degree	1	2	3	4	5	6	7	8
Note Name	C	D	E	F	G	A	B	C
Chord Formula	1		3		#5			
Notes in Chord	C		E		G#			

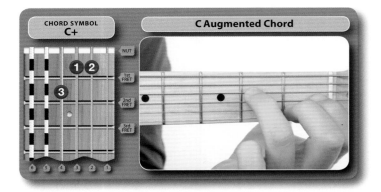

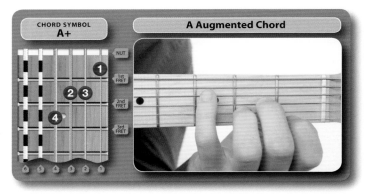

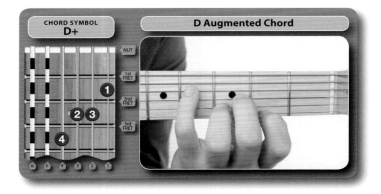

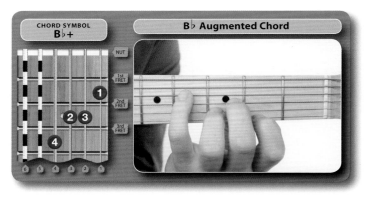

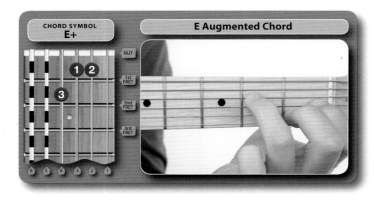

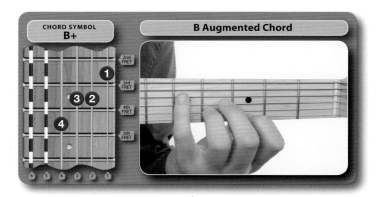

Diminished Chords

Diminished chords are constructed from the **1st, flat 3rd, flat 5th** & **double flat 7th** degrees of the Major scale.

e.g. **C°**

Scale Degree	1	2	3	4	5	6	7	8
Note Name	C	D	E	F	G	A	B	C
Chord Formula	1		♭3		♭5	♭♭7		
Notes in Chord	C		E♭		G♭	7♭♭		

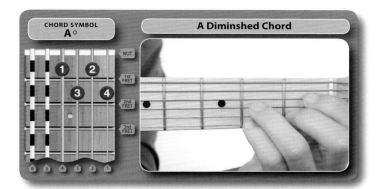

CHORD SYMBOL A° — A Diminshed Chord

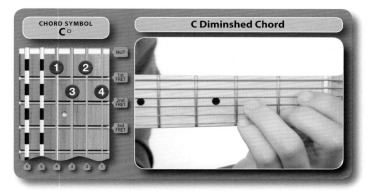

CHORD SYMBOL C° — C Diminshed Chord

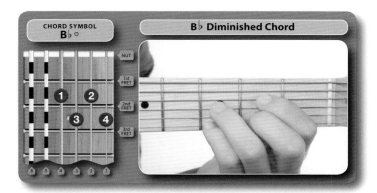

CHORD SYMBOL B♭° — B♭ Diminshed Chord

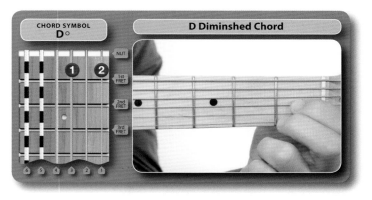

CHORD SYMBOL D° — D Diminshed Chord

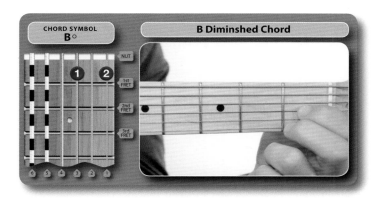

CHORD SYMBOL B° — B Diminshed Chord

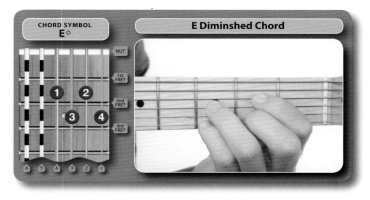

CHORD SYMBOL E° — E Diminshed Chord

Index of Musical Terms

'a' – annular finger (ring finger). As used for identifying the right hand fingers in fingerpicking patterns.

Accent — a sign, > used to indicate a predominant note or beat.

Accidental — a sign used to show a temporary change in pitch of a note (i.e. sharp ♯, flat ♭, double sharp 𝄪, double flat ♭♭, or natural ♮). The sharps or flats in a key signature are **not regarded as accidentals.**

Ad lib — to be played at the performer's own discretion.

Allegretto — moderately fast.

Allegro — fast and lively.

Anacrusis — a note or notes occurring before the first bar of music (also called 'lead-in' notes).

Andante — an easy walking pace.

Arpeggio — the playing of a chord in single note fashion.

Bar — a division of music occurring between two bar lines (also called a 'measure').

Bar chord — a chord played with one finger lying across all six strings.

Bar line — a vertical line drawn across the staff which divides the music into equal sections called bars.

Bass — the lower regions of pitch in general. On keyboard, the notes to the left of the keyboard.

Bend — a technique which involves pushing a string upwards (or downward), which raises the pitch of the fretted note being played.

Blues Scale — consisting of the Ī, ♭IIĪ, ĪV̄, ♭V̄, V̄ and ♭VIĪ notes relative to the major scale.

Capo — a device placed across the neck of a guitar to allow a key change without alteration of the chord shapes.

Chord — a combination of three or more different notes played together.

Chord progression — a series of chords played as a musical unit (e.g. as in a song).

Chromatic scale — a scale ascending and descending in semitones.

e.g. **C** chromatic scale:

ascending:	C	C♯	D	D♯	E	F	F♯	G	G♯	A	A♯	B	C
descending:	C	B	B♭	A	A♭	G	G♭	F	E	E♭	D	D♭	C

Clef — a sign placed at the beginning of each staff of music which fixes the location of a particular note on the staff, and hence the location of all other notes, e.g.

Coda — an ending section of music, signified by the sign ⊕.

Common time — and indication of $\frac{4}{4}$ time — four quarter note beats per bar (also indicated by **C**)

Compound time — occurs when the beat falls on a dotted note, which is thus divisible by 3 e.g. $\frac{6}{8}$ $\frac{9}{8}$ $\frac{12}{8}$

D.C al fine — a repeat from the beginning of the piece, up to the word 'fine'.

Dot — a sign placed after a note indicating that its time value is extended by a half. e.g. ♩ = 2 counts   ♩. = 3 counts

Double Bar Line — two vertical lines close together, indicating the end of a piece, or section thereof.

Double Flat — a sign (♭♭) which lowers the pitch of a note by one tone.

Double Sharp — a sign (𝄪) which raises the pitch of a note by one tone.

D.S. al fine — a repeat from the sign (indicated thus 𝄋) to the word 'fine'.

Duration — the time value of each note.

Dynamics — the varying degrees of softness (indicated by the term 'piano') and loudness (indicated by the term 'forte') in music.

Eighth note — a note with the value of half a beat in $\frac{4}{4}$ time, indicated thus ♪ (also called a quaver).

Eighth note rest — indicating half a beat of silence is written: ♪

Enharmonic — describes the difference in notation, but not in pitch, of two notes: e.g.

F♯ or G♭

Fermata — a sign, ⌢, used to indicate that a note or chord is held to the player's own discretion (also called a 'pause sign').

First and second endings — signs used where two different endings occur. On the first time through ending one is played (indicated by the bracket ⌐1.⌐); then the progression is repeated and ending two is played (indicated ⌐2.⌐).

Flat — a sign, (♭) used to lower the pitch of a note by one semitone.

Form — the plan or layout of a song, in relation to the sections it contains; e.g. Binary form, containing an "A" section and a "B" section (AB). Ternary form, containing an A section and a B section, and then a repeat of the A section (ABA). The verse/chorus relationship in songs is an example of form.

Forte — loud. Indicated by the sign *f*.

Half note — a note with the value of two beats in $\frac{4}{4}$ time, indicated thus: ♩ (also called a minim). The **half note rest**, indicating two beats of silence, is written: ▬ **on the** third staff line.

Hammer on — sounding a note by using only the left hand fingers (also called a 'slur').

Harmonics — a chime like sound created by lightly touching a vibrating string at certain points along the fretboard.

Harmony — the simultaneous sounding of two or more different notes.

'i' — index finger. As used for identifying the right hand fingers in fingerpicking patterns.

Improvise — to perform spontaneously; i.e. not from memory or from a written copy.

Interval — the distance between any two notes of different pitches.

Key — describes the notes used in a composition in regards to the major or minor scale from which they are taken; e.g. a piece 'in the key of C major' describes the melody, chords, etc. as predominantly consisting of the notes **C, D, E, F, G, A,** and **B** — i.e. from the **C** scale.

Key signature — a sign placed at the beginning of each stave of music, directly after the clef, to indicate the key of a piece. The sign consists of a certain number of sharps or flats, which represent the sharps or flats found in the scale of the piece's key. E.g.

indicates a scale with **F♯** and **C♯**, which is **D** major; **D E F♯ G A B C♯ D.** Therefore the key is **D** major.

Lead-In — same as anacrusis (also called a pick-up).

Legato — smoothly, well connected.

Leger lines — small horizontal lines upon which notes are written when their pitch is either above or below the range of the staff, e.g.

Lyric — words that accompany a melody.

'm' — middle finger. As used for identifying the right hand fingers in fingerpicking patterns.

Major Pentatonic Scale — a 5 tone scale based on the interval sequence, $T, T, T\frac{1}{2}, T, T\frac{1}{2}$.

Major scale — a series of eight notes in alphabetical order based on the interval sequence tone - tone - semitone - tone - tone - tone - semitone, giving the familiar sound **do re mi fa so la ti do**.

Melody — a succession of notes of varying pitch and duration, and having a recognizable musical shape.

Metronome — a device which indicates the number of beats per minute, and which can be adjusted in accordance to the desired tempo.

e.g. **MM** (Maelzel Metronome) ♩ = 60 — indicates 60 quarter note beats per minute.

Moderato — at a moderate pace.

Modulation — the changing of key within a song (or chord progression).

Natural — a sign (♮)used to cancel out the effect of a sharp or flat. The word is also used to describe the notes **A**, **B**, **C**, **D**, **E**, **F** and **G**; e.g. 'the natural notes'.

Notation — the written representation of music, by means of symbols (music on a staff), letters (as in chord and note names) and diagrams (as in chord illustrations.)

Note — a single sound with a given pitch and duration.

Octave — the distance between any given note with a set frequency, and another note with exactly double that frequency. Both notes will have the same letter name;

Open chord — a chord that contains at least one open string.

'p' — primary finger (thumb). As used for identifying the right hand fingers in fingerpicking patterns.

Passing note — connects two melody notes which are a third or less apart. A passing note usually occurs on an unaccented beat of the bar.

Phrase — a small group of notes forming a recognizable unit within a melody.

Pitch — the sound produced by a note, determined by the frequency of the string vibrations. The pitch relates to a note being referred to as 'high' or 'low'.

Pivot finger — a finger which remains in position while the other fingers move, when changing chords.

Plectrum — a small object (often of a triangular shape) made of plastic which is used to pick or strum the strings of a guitar.

Position — a term used to describe the location of the left hand on the fretboard. The left hand position is determined by the fret location of the first finger, e.g. The 1st position refers to the 1st to 4th frets. The 3rd position refers to the 3rd to 6th frets and so on.

Quarter note — a note with the value of one beat in $\frac{4}{4}$ time, indicated thus (also called a crotchet). The quarter note rest, indicating one beat of silence, is written: .

Relative — a term used to describe the relationship between a major and minor key which share the same key signature; e.g. G major and E minor are relative keys both sharing the F♯ key signature.

Repeat signs — used to indicate a repeat of a section of music, by means of two dots placed before a double bar line:

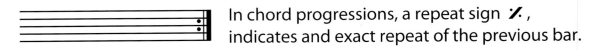

In chord progressions, a repeat sign ✗ , indicates and exact repeat of the previous bar.

Rest — the notation of an absence of sound in music.

Rest stroke — where the finger, after picking the string, comes to rest on the next string (for accenting the note).

Rhythm — the pattern of strong and weak pulses in a piece or section of music.

Riff — a pattern of notes that is repeated throughout a progression (song).

Root note — the note after which a chord or scale is named.

Scale Tone Chords — chords which are constructed from notes within a given scale.

Semitone — the smallest interval used in conventional music. On guitar, it is a distance of one fret.

Sharp — a sign (♯) used to raise the pitch of a note by one semitone.

Simple time — occurs when the beat falls on an undotted note, which is thus divisible by two.

Sixteenth note — a note with the value of a quarter of a beat in $\frac{4}{4}$ time, indicated as such ♪ (also called a semiquaver). The sixteenth note rest, indicating a quarter of a beat of silence, is written: ⅞

Slide — a technique which involves a finger moving along the string to its new note. The finger maintains pressure on the string, so that a continuous sound is produced.

Slur — sounding a note by using only the left hand fingers. (An ascending slur is also called a 'hammer on'; a descending slur is also called a 'pull off.')

Staccato — to play short and detached. Indicated by a dot placed above the note:

Staff — five parallel lines together with four spaces, upon which music is written.

Syncopation — the placing of an accent on a normally unaccented beat. e.g.:

$\frac{4}{4}$ 1 2̇ 3 4̇ $\frac{3}{4}$ 1 + 2̇ + 3 +̇

Tablature — a system of writing music which represents the position of the player's fingers (not the pitch of the notes, but their position on the guitar). A chord diagram is a type of tablature. Notes can also be written using tablature thus:

Music Notation

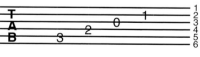
Tablature

Tempo — the speed of a piece.

Tie — a curved line joining two or more notes of the same pitch, where the second note(s) is not played, but its time value is added to that of the first note.

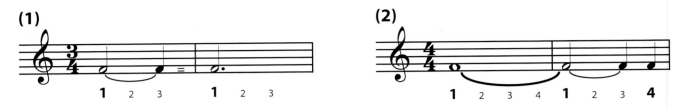

Timbre — a quality which distinguishes a note produced on one instrument from the same note produced on any other instrument (also called 'tone colour'). A given note on the guitar will sound different (and therefore distinguishable) from the same pitched note on piano, violin, flute etc. There is usually also a difference in timbre from one guitar to another.

Time signature — a sign at the beginning of a piece which indicates, by means of figures, the number of beats per bar (top figure), and the type of note receiving one beat (bottom figure).

Tone — a distance of two frets; i.e. the equivalent of two semitones.

Transposition — the process of changing music from one key to another.

Treble — the upper regions of pitch in general.

Treble clef — a sign placed at the beginning of the staff to fix the pitch of the notes placed on it. The treble clef (also called 'G clef') is placed so that the second line indicates a G note:

← **G line**

Tremolo (pick tremolo) — a technique involving rapid pick movement on a given note.

Triplet — a group of three notes played in the same time as two notes of the same kind.

Vibrato — a technique which involves pushing a string up and down, like a rapid series of short bends.

Wedge mark — indicates pick direction; e.g:

$$V = \text{down pick}, \quad \Lambda = \text{up pick}$$

Whole note — a note with the value of four beats in $\frac{4}{4}$ time, indicated thus ○ (also called a semibreve).

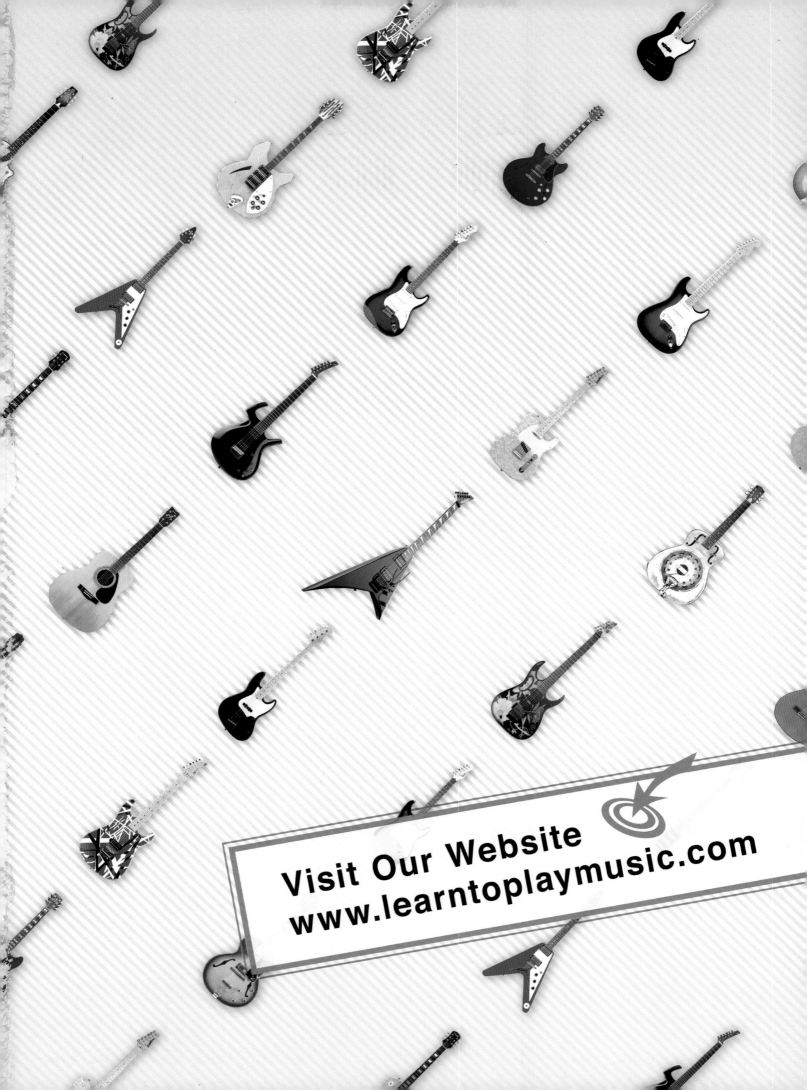